When The Wind Blows

James Robe

AMBASSADOR PRODUCTIONS LTD.,
241 UPPER NEWTONARDS ROAD,
BELFAST BT4 3JF
455 Great Western Road,
Glasgow G12 8HH

Copyright © 1985 Ambassador Productions Ltd.
ISBN 0 907927 07 6
Printed and bound in Great Britain
by Forsyth Middleton & Co. Ltd., Kilsyth.

FOREWORD

I am very happy indeed to write a brief Foreword to this stirring account of the revival at Kilsyth and Cambuslang in 1742. The retention of the fine Introductory Essay by Robert Buchanan, Glasgow, makes any apology for the events the book brings before us unnecessary. All I need do is commend it in the warmest terms to the Christian public of today.

To live through a genuine revival of religion, when God's Spirit is poured out plentifully and moves powerfully upon a church and community, is surely one of the most enriching and blessed experiences God ever bestows upon His people. Sadly, it is not one of which the present generation in Scotland has any first hand knowledge.

The ministers most intimately involved, James Robe, Kilsyth and William McCulloch, Cambuslang, were effective publicists of the amazing work of God amongst their people and were wise enough to keep a contemporary record of what went on. Not only so, they issued a 'monthly history' while the revival was going on which was then collated and published in 1744. Their account thus brings us into immediate contact with the movement and helps us visualise what living through a revival would be like. This is the great value of the book for us. Few things, in my view, are better calculated to stimulate interest in and prayer for a work of revival in our land than the contemporary record of what God has done in the past, and the stories of the lives and the lives saved.

It is surely significant, also, that the revival brought before us here was, itself, preceded by the publication of a history of the revivals in that very area about a century earlier. And it is a fact that an edition of this book, published in 1840, was followed soon afterwards by yet another revival in the Kilsyth district under the passionate, evangelistic preaching of William Chalmers Burns.

It would be a signal, and by no means impossible, manifestation of God's rich mercy and grace if its reappearance now were to be the precursor of yet another outpouring of the same Spirit upon us.

J. DOUGLAS MACMILLAN
Free Church College, Edinburgh.
February 1985

CONTENTS

INTRODUCTORY ESSAY

THERE is something cheering and delightful in the very word *Revival*. It calls up to the mind a crowd of associations, all of them of the most pleasing and exhilarating kind. If used with reference to the human frame, it suggests the idea of returning health: of pain giving place to ease, and weakness to strength: of fear yielding to hope, and anxiety to joy. If used with reference to public affairs, it presents a picture of returning prosperity: of confidence restored, and commerce flowing again into its wonted channels: of industry rewarded and comfort diffused: of want and discontent, and all those other evils which the previous stagnation and disorder had produced, disappearing from the land. If used with reference to nature itself, it fills the imagination with sweet thoughts of spring: a brighter sun quickening all things, out of the decay and dreariness of winter, into life and loveliness once more: the desolate fields putting on their verdant mantle: the leafless woods bursting forth into fresh and fragrant foliage, and made tuneful with the voice of birds: the bright ploughshare glancing between the opening furrows — the busy husbandman pursuing his cheerful toil: Every heart gladdened by the prospect, sure though distant, of that bounteous harvest by which the year shall at length be crowned.

1

How strange that to many minds this word, so pleasing in every other connection, should not only lose all its charm but become utterly distasteful and offensive when used with reference to religion! By every well constituted mind the revival of an immortal soul, under the power of Divine truth, ought surely to be regarded as an event unspeakably more interesting and delightful than any revival affecting only the temporal estate of man. The body may revive and the gloom of the sick chamber be dispelled, and the saddened countenances of friends be brightened into joy; but a few years have only to run their course in order that the same sick chamber must be anew prepared, and that mourning friends must again be gathered around. The *soul,* once revived by the Spirit of God, can never die! When Peter presented Dorcas alive, revived by the power of Christ, to the saints and widows who filled the upper chamber at Joppa, weeping over her decease, it is indeed delightful to think of the glad surprise that must suddenly have beamed from every eye and dried up every tear. But that company nevertheless must ere long, in the common course of nature, have reassembled to behold their friend and benefactor, in whose restoration they now rejoiced, finally carried to the cold and silent grave. When, on the other hand, the Lord Jesus standing by the pallet on which lay the man that was brought in before him, sick of the palsy, said unto him, "Son, be of good cheer, thy sins be forgiven thee," the germ of life eternal was that instant implanted in his soul. His bodily frame might indeed again become powerless under the pressure of a new disease, but his undying spirit had been healed for ever of the deadly disease of sin.

And if this consideration should invest a religious revival with a character of profoundest interest and importance, viewed simply in its bearing on the condition and destiny of an individual soul, much more surely when viewed in its wider bearing on a community, on a country, on the world.

If we look around us on the *community* in which we live, how many scenes and objects meet the eye fitted to shock the sensibilities and wound the feelings of every benevolent heart. The squalid poverty, the want and nakedness, in which hundreds and thousands of families are dragging out a wretched existence; the crowds of neglected children growing up in ignorance and vice; the domestic misery which embitters so many homes; the drunkenness, the profaneness, the profligacy which so disgracefully abound; what friend of humanity can survey these things without longing for some means by which they may at least be mitigated if not wholly removed? And no doubt the philanthropists of this world are ready with their schemes of social improvement. One has his proposal for encreasing the means of employment, another thinks the cure will be found in a rise of wages — a third confidently anticipates the same result from a greater diffusion of secular knowledge, while a different class, of sterner and more practical minds, place their reliance on an extended police and a more rigorous exercise of criminal justice. But who that looks beneath the surface of things — that is accustomed to trace up effects to their cause, can fail to perceive that all these devices are but so many vain attempts to daub the wall of the social edifice with untempered mortar, concealing perhaps for a time but not in the least removing, the rottenness that is hidden within? The physical disorders that so extensively afflict society, together with the whole train of vices by which they are accompanied, flow out of a diseased moral and spiritual condition. "I have been young, said the Psalmist, and now am old, yet have I not seen the righteous forsaken nor his seed begging bread." "Godliness, said the Apostle, is profitable unto all things, having promise of the life *now* is," as well as of "that which is to come." It is irreligion which is the pregnant and pernicious source of poverty and profligacy and crime; and nothing but a religious revival can have power to chase those evils from the many wretched lanes of this mighty city, and to bring back industry and comfort, virtue and happiness, to the dark and desolate dwellings which are now tenanted only by misery and vice.

If from the community we give the eye a wider range, and embrace within the sweep of its observation the country at large, how much, on this ampler field, do we daily descry to grieve, and even to alarm, every patriotic mind? *Infidelity* busily and boldly assailing, not only the evidences of revealed truth but the very first principles of morals; no longer, as in former times, concealing itself amid the folds of subtle speculation, and addressing itself to men of learning and science — but coming forth in its naked deformity among the lower orders of the people, and proclaiming with unabashed visage the most revolting practical abominations: *Popery,* seemingly the enemy and the opposite, but in truth the sworn friend and natural ally of infidelity, successfully struggling to recover its ancient and baleful ascendancy, fatal alike to the temporal prosperity and eternal welfare of mankind: While between the two, and extending a friendly hand to each, stands *religious liberalism,* scornfully indifferent to all diversities of creed, and priding itself in its insane and impious attempt to bind society in harmony and peace, by inducing all to break those bands and cast away those cords by which the Prince of peace has sought to unite them, at once to each other and to their God and Father in heaven. As if when men of all forms of faith had agreed to build one common altar and on

4

that altar to offer up *Truth* as a sacrifice, that *then* would be the time, over the ashes of that sacrifice, to swear vows of mutual reconciliation and friendship never again to be broken. And while so many poisonous influences are thus at work upon the public mind, unsettling the religious convictions and perverting or deadening the moral sense of the people, at the same time that nothing at all corresponding to their immensely increased numbers has been done to provide them with the means of sound religious instruction, is it surprising that a spirit of insubordination, breaking out at times into lawless and fearful outrage, should be found extensively diffused and actively at work in so many districts of the land? Politicians, many of them see indeed the fact, and the more reflecting of them, tremble perhaps at the dangers it involves, but how few of them, of any party, ascribe it to its proper cause, or understand and are prepared to apply the only remedy by which a better order of things can ever be permanently restored. Wordly politicians have no doubt, and that in abundance, their schemes of national improvement. The removal of some tax that presses injuriously on the springs of trade; the opening up of new fields for commercial enterprise; the drawing off of our surplus population to colonize distant regions of the earth; an increase or a diminution of popular influence in our political system; a new law to lower the price of agri-cultural produce; penitentiaries, mechanics' institutes, 'useful knowledge' societies, in a word, schemes as numerous and as various as are the diversities of the human mind itself, are all propounded, and with equal confidence, by their respective advocates; and each is held up as the grand panacea which is to heal the nation's maladies and to ensure that universal contentment and prosperity which all alike profess to be longing to secure.

5

But while wordly politicians are busily contriving, or vehemently demanding the application of their endless and often antagonist specifics, it is forgotten where the true secret of a nation's welfare and a nation's greatness lies. They overlook that fundamental truth recorded in the word of God, that "righteousness alone exalteth a nation," and that there is no other means by which that righteousness can be either produced or preserved, but the means God in his infinite wisdom and goodness has himself ordained, namely, the lessons and the ordinances of pure and undefiled religion. Can any one for an instant suppose that serious danger to the public peace could possibly arise among a people, universally trained in the fear of God. Had due pains been taken to establish that grand controling principle — the true basis of all moral obligation — in the hearts of the teeming multitudes who throng our great cities and manu-facturing villages, no one would have needed to fear the torch of the incendiary nor the insurrectionary violence of an inflamed and misguided populace. The voice which hushed the tempest on the sea of Galilee, when the labouring bark was ready to perish amid the angry waves, is that alone which is of power sufficient "to still the tumults of the people." That voice heard in each home, as the family bible is reverently opened at the morning and evening services of domestic devotion; that voice mingling with the daily instructions of the school, giving line upon line, and precept upon precept, to the impressible mind of youth; that voice breathing in solemn accents from sabbath to sabbath, amid the assembled congregation in the sanctuary: speaking as it does with demonstration to the understanding, with authority to the conscience, and with persuasive power to the heart, will give a moral tone to society which no arts of mere secular legislation can ever impart. It is this blessed influence of religion, which, reconciling even the poorest to the hardships of their lot in time, by opening up to them the glorious prospects of a happy eternity, will alone suffice to chase away the sullen discontent with which the humbler are so generally found frowning on the higher orders of society; and to bind all classes together in mutual kindness and sympathy, as all equally in need of, and all equally depending on, the mercy of a common Redeemer. Let a branch cut from this tree be cast into the bitterest waters, and straightway they will become sweet and salutary. It is therefore to a religious revival throughout the nation, we must look, as the only effectual means of securing us against the manifold dangers which menace the public weal; and of giving permanence and stability to all those time-honoured institutions, with whose preservation is identified the prosperity, perhaps the existence, of the greatest empire in the world. Then should "violence no more be heard in our land, wasting nor destruction within our borders;" but men should call our "walls salvation and our gates praise." Then should we be called Hephzibah, and our land Beulah, because the Lord delighted in it — because then it should be wedded to the Lord.

But once more, if from the *country* we rise to the survey of the *world* — if ascending the lofty eminence which is occupied by the genius of history, we review the annals of our race; or setting out with the traveller, we bring the eye of observation to bear on the existing condition of mankind — what a mournful picture is presented to the reflecting mind! Over by far the larger portion of that wide expanse, what does either the past or the present exhibit, but "darkness covering the earth and gross darkness the people"? Millions upon millions of our fellow-creatures, possessed of the same rational, moral, and immortal nature with ourselves, sunk to the

7

level of the beasts that perish; ignorant alike of their origin and of their end — "changing the glory of the incorruptible Jehovah into an image made like to corruptible man, and to birds and four-footed beasts and creeping things." Humanity shudders even to think of the scenes that are daily witnessed in these dark places of the earth, which are full of the habitations of horrid cruelty. To see the wretched inhabitant of magnificent India standing for years with his shrivelled arm, out-stretched and immovable, beneath the burning sun, or piercing with savage violence his own flesh as he dances with frantic vehemence before his frightful divinity, or lying down to be crushed like a worm beneath the wheels of the idol-car at Juggernaut; to see the poor degraded African, prostrate and trembling before the *Fetish,* the misshapen and senseless image which his own hands have made; to see the ferocious New Zealander feeding on human flesh, and that too with the conviction that there is something religious in this unnatural and monstrous feast, how does the very heart sicken at spectacles like these! The man of European refinement and intelligence feels almost ashamed of his own nature when he sees it thus brutalized. And yet what is it that makes him to differ? Nothing but the religion of the Gospel — the religion of that blessed Jesus who is the light of the world, and whose word wherever it is known and embraced, has never failed to bring light to them that were in darkness and in the region and shadow of death. If we pass in review before us all the nations of the earth, and fix on that one of their number in which peace and order and civilization, comfort and freedom and knowledge most widely reign, we shall find it to be the very nation in which true religion is most extensively diffused. Or if we fix, on the other hand, on the nation which of all others is sunk deepest in darkness, degradation, and misery; where the rights of man are most habitually trampled under foot, where both his mental and bodily condition are most abject and debased, we shall find it to be just that nation which has stood farthest removed from all contact and communication with the religion of Christ; into which no ray, direct or traditionary, of its living and life-giving light has ever shone. Does not this one fact tell us, and that with the irresistible force of a demonstration, how and how alone the misery in which the earth "groaneth and travaileth" until now, is to be done away; that it is in the *revival of religion* we must seek for the means of regenerating the world? As we have worldly philanthropists full of schemes for the improvement of the community; and worldly politicians as full of schemes for the improvement of the country, so have we worldly cosmopolites, citizens of the world as they delight to be called, whose zeal for humanity professes to have no limits narrower than the globe, and who are fondly dreaming of a millennium in which the Gospel is to have no share. It is to the diffusion of knowledge they look for the reformation of mankind. The infidel theory, contradicted alike by the explicit testimony of Scripture and the ascertained facts of history, on which they proceed, is that: this man started in the race of being at the lowest point of intelligence and virtue, and that by a series of progressive evolutions he has been continually advancing, under the operation of mere natural causes, towards the destined perfection of his nature. Scripture on the contrary declares of man, as of all the other works of God, that he came forth from the hands of his Maker "very good" — enstamped with his Maker's image. And that from this high original elevation, there has been subsequently a constant tendency downwards to ignorance and depravity, wherever that tendency has not been arrested and borne back by the new influence of that economy of grace under which fallen man was placed. In conformity with the view thus given on the immovable authority of revelation, history, so far as we can dimly trace its course up to the cloudy heights of remote antiquity, proclaims the same truth. Assyria, India, and Egypt, the most ancient kingdoms of which any authentic memorials have come down, were then evidently in possession of a learning and refinement, which in later ages were nearly altogether lost and forgotten. If there has been a progress going on, as in a certain sense and within certain limits undoubtedly is true, that progress has been identical with and uniformly dependent on the advancement of true religion. And while the infidel theorist points to the arms, and the ships, and the commerce of this great kingdom, as spreading themselves abroad over the whole habitable earth, and carrying the arts and sciences of European civilization in their train, he wilfully or proudly overlooks the source of that moral and intellectual energy to which Britain owes the mighty influence it is thus exerting on the world. He forgets that Christianity, humanizing, refining, and elevating the heart and mind, is the well-spring at once of our national resources and of our national renown. And if forgetting this ourselves, we shall presume to say, 'by the strength of our own hand we have done it, and by our widsom, for we are prudent,' — then shall irreligion like a canker eat out the vitals of our strength, and the power and glory under which we now sit secure, shall wither like the prophet's gourd. Not only does the infidel forget all this, but he forgets that neither our fleets nor our armies, our merchants nor our men of science, can reform the world. They can indeed lay down a way on which a higher and nobler influence must go forth; they can remove the obstacles, and this doubtless under a gracious overruling

Providence is the office they are destined to perform, levelling, so to speak, the mountains, and filling up the valleys that a high road may be prepared on which the chariot of the everlasting Gospel shall run till it encircle the earth. And it is when in obedience to that gospel-call, the blinded heathens shall everywhere be found casting their idols to the moles and to the bats, and saying to one another, "Come ye and let us go up to the mountain of the Lord, to the house of the God of Jacob, and He will teach us of his ways, and we will walk in his paths:" it is then that men will at length beat their swords into ploughshares and their spears into pruning hooks, that nation shall not lift up sword against nation, neither shall they learn war any more: it is then "the wolf shall dwell with the lamb and the leopard shall lie down with the kid, and the calf and the young lion and the fatling together, and a little child shall lead them. Because the earth shall be full of the knowledge of the glory of the Lord as the waters cover the sea!"

Whether then we look at the community, the country, or the world, what urgent cause has the church continually to cry with the Psalmist — "Wilt thou not revive us again, that thy people may rejoice in thee?" Even if we looked no farther and no higher than to man's condition in time, how many arguments does that condition, as it now exists, present, all proclaiming with one voice the unspeakable importance and necessity of a religious revival. Do the wise and enlightened mourn over abounding ignorance and folly, the just over abounding crime, the virtuous over abounding vice, the humane over abounding misery? Do the citizen, the patriot, the lover of mankind, throughout the respective spheres within which their observation turns, perceive every day a thousand wrongs which they sigh to see redressed, a thousand evils which they long to see removed: it is relig-

11

ion they must call to their aid. It is this which alone can make righteousness to run down our streets as waters and judgement as a river: it is this alone which can make the land peaceful, prosperous, and secure, it is this alone which can give to the earth its millennial reign of tranquillity and joy.

But when from the narrow confines of time, we stretch out our view into the boundless regions of eternity, and think of the millions of our fellow men now living in misery and sin, as hurrying onwards to a state of endless and unutterable woe — how should every man that knows the worth of an imperishable soul burn with fervent desire to save these perishing multitudes from so dreadful a destiny. And what but the coldness and deadness of religion among us, is it, that enables us to look on at the state of things which thus exists around us, whether in the community or the country or the world, with so much cold and heartless unconcern? Were the spirit of the Gospel active and energetic within us, were the tide of its devine charity flowing warm and vigorous in our veins, we would be giving the Lord no rest from our importunate petitions — saying, "Awake, awake; put on strength, O arm of the Lord: awake as in the ancient days, as in the generations of old!" And does not the very fact that we are so little moved by the sight of the desolations of many generations which overspread our city, our country, and the world, marking as it does the low ebb to which religious conviction and feeling have sunk in ourselves, constitute the most impressive reason for taking this prayer into our lips, "God be merciful unto us and bless us, and cause thy face to shine upon us, *that* thy way may be known upon the earth, and thy saving health among all nations"? A revival of religion in God's own people must precede and prepare for a revival of religion in the world. It is when the Son of man is walking among the golden candlesticks, and feeding the lamps with fresh oil, that their light, clear and strong, will penetrate farthest into the surrounding darkness. It is when the waters of life are welling out most copiously from the sanctuary that their streams will spread most widely abroad over the adjacent wilderness. And accordingly it is in immediate connection with a religious revival, in which they that make mention of the Lord shall not keep silence, but shall give Him no rest — that He hath promised to establish Jerusalem and make it a praise in the earth.

In the preceding part of this essay, we have set forth some of the considerations that should make a religious revival the object of deep interest and earnest prayer to the Church at all periods of her history as the church militant, and in every situation in which she can be placed. The happiness of men on earth and their everlasting blessedness in heaven, and, through these, the glory of God our Saviour, all conduce to exhort us without ceasing to this comprehensive supplication: "Oh Lord, wilt thou not revive us again, that thy people may rejoice in thee!" At the same time it must be obvious to the reflecting mind that in the church's history a season will occasionally come round, when that unusually abundant outpouring of the Holy Spirit which is at once the cause and the characteristic of a revival is more than ordinarily needed, and when therefore it ought to be, with more than common urgency, sought. When the Church has come into straits: when for her sins she has been visited with a day of rebuke and blasphemy: when by reason of abounding iniquity the love of many of her own professing friends is waxing cold, and when the energy and the confidence of the adversary are in the same measure and on the same ground increased: in a word, when the enemy on every side is coming in like a flood, it is then there should be the loudest call, as then is there the most pressing necessity, for the Spirit of the Lord to lift up a standard against him. It was when Judah of old had gone into captivity: when the Lord had thus afflicted Zion for the multitude of her transgressions and had suffered her adversaries to become the chief and her enemies, to prosper, it was for that trying season, the Holy Spirit dictated this course, saying, "Arise, cry in the night: in the beginning of the watches pour out thine heart like water before the face of the Lord, lift up thy hands toward him for the life of thy young children that faint for hunger in the top of every street." (Jer. ii, 19.) And the burden of Zion's prayer was to be this: "Wherefore dost thou forget us for ever and forsake us so long time? Turn thou us unto thee, O Lord, and we shall be turned: renew our days as of old." (Jer. v, 20, 21.). Without such a reviving there could, in a crisis of that kind, be no hope for the church at all. Unless the Spirit were then to come down as rain upon the mown grass, as showers that water and refresh the earth, it could have nothing remaining for it but to decay and die. It is not only that in the face of these accumulated dangers it could have no reasonable prospect of enlargement, but that, on the contrary, its already narrow limits must be contracted more and more, until, buried and lost beneath the flood of error and wickedness, the place that knew it should know it no more.

In passing therefore, as we are now doing, from the *general* to the *special* reasons which render a religious revival important, from those reasons which exist at all times, to those other and additional reasons whose force is derived from the peculiar circumstances in which the church may happen at a given time to be placed, we are naturally led to enquire how far any of those special reasons exist at the present day. There is certainly no

14

good to be gained, by drawing, and holding up to view, an exaggerated picture of the dangers with which religion is assailed; but neither is there any wisdom in under-rating and despising them. To state the case then in the most guarded form, it may surely be affirmed without fear of challenge from any intelligent Christian, that religion is very far indeed from being in a satisfactory state among us. That thousands and tens of thousands of the inhabitants of this kingdom are living in utter ignorance of divine truth, and in total estrangement from divine ordinances, is too painfully notorious to be denied. That not thousands, but millions of our fellow-subjects, especially in the neighbouring island, are the blinded votaries of antichrist is, unhappily, alike indisputable. That this melancholy state of things should be found in a nation privileged with a pure Gospel for three hundred years, must beyond all question involve a guilt and a responsibility of no ordinary kind. It would be difficult and might prove invidious to attempt to distribute that responsibility and guilt, in their just proportions, among the various parties on whom they undoubtedly lie. But there can be no reason why we should hesitate to affirm that the churches more immediately intrusted with the religious instruction of the nation, have much cause in this matter deeply to humble themselves in the sight of God. Had the Church of Ireland since the dawn of the Reformation been earnestly contending for the pure faith, once delivered to the saints, and then restored to that long benighted land; had He whose eyes are as a flame of fire and his feet like fine brass, had cause to say of her — "I know thy works and charity and service and faith, and thy patience and thy works," — we cannot believe that there the dark and degrading dominion of the man of sin would so long and so extensively have been allowed to prevail. And had the

15

Churches of England and of Scotland, during all that long lapse of time, been "doing their first works," — been labouring with the freshness and fidelity of their early youth, surely so many "waste places" could not have been suffered to appear. Above all, and on this it becomes us more pointedly to dwell, because it is with the confession of our own sins we have chiefly to do, had the church of our fathers never forgotten her first love — had the holy zeal for the cause of God which distinguished her earlier years, and which shone so brightly in the dark night of persecution, which once and again came down upon her path, continued to inspire with equal ardour her ministers and elders and people in later times, our beloved country would not now have presented the mournful spectacle which too many of its towns and parishes exhibit — homes in hundreds in which family religion is unknown, and in which children receive no lesson that can ever lead them unto God — Sabbaths profaned — the services of the sanctuary unheeded or even despised — unaquaintance with the Bible and the Catechism, once accounted even by the humblest, a reproach, now too common in many places to excite a remark: and as the fruit of this religious declension, a growth of vice and crime which have already grievously dishonoured our country's once venerated name.

It would have been strange indeed, if the sinful neglect of duty out of which these evils have sprung, had not prepared for us a time of trouble and rebuke. It is the righteous and immutable law of Divine providence, "Thine own wickedness shall correct thee and thy backslidings shall reprove thee." And the end of that law is, to make the offenders know, that "it is an evil thing and bitter that they have forsaken the Lord their God and that His fear has not been in them." In a former part of this essay, allusion was already made, to the lamentable progress and threatening aspects of Popery and Infidelity, and to the united force with which both are directing their energies, now to sap and undermine, now openly to assail, both the religion and the religious institutions of the land. And when it is borne in mind that from the causes above noticed so large a portion of our people have been sinfully suffered to fall aside, from the pale of religious influence altogether, no one can fail to see how ample are the materials, both for the Infidel and the Romanist, which have thus been prepared to their hand, and which, were an offended God to let loose His judgments might come to be wielded with terrific power against the peace and safety of the church of Christ.

But it is not *without* only that danger to the cause of religion exists. An army can look out from their encampment, on the gathering legions of the enemy undismayed, so long as mutual confidence reigns among themselves. But when discord and division are pervading and paralysing their own ranks, making each man doubt and distrust his fellow, it is then their strength departs and they are ready to be given for a prey. And who can doubt that in some at least of its features, this picture is but too painfully descriptive of the existing condition of the different religious denominations of whom, taken collectively, Christ's church is in this kingdom composed? When the Infidel and the Romanist are shaking hands, and the men of no religion are willingly joined in their counsels, what alas! do we discover among the friends of God's cause and truth? Instead of casting away all regard to minor differences and joining in a solemn league and covenant to maintain and uphold the banner of the cross, they are spending their energies in fatal contests among themselves! When

17

one first turns to look at these discouraging symptoms, partaking as they do so largely of something which at least greatly resembles the judicial blindness which commonly precedes a judgment, a feeling, almost approaching to despondency, is ready to take possession of the mind. A closer observation, however, serves not a little to revive the Christian's hope and to diminish, though not certainly to dissipate his fears. Amid all the unpromising appearances which have now been described, there can be distinctly discerned a visible and vigorous growth of genuine religion. It is this *begun revival,* this increase of heart — warm evangelical preaching in our pulpits, and of personal piety among our people, manifesting themselves in a livelier concern for the honour and advancement of the Redeemer's kingdom both at home and abroad, it is this which seems plainly to warrant us in believing that the Lord has a purpose of mercy towards our church and nation still. It is this which encourages us to say with Manoah, "If the Lord were pleased to destroy us he would not have received a burnt-offering and a meat-offering at our hands." If then these first drops of the shower have sufficed to impart to us that measure of strength we now enjoy, how blessed would it be if our watchers, like the servant of Elijah, when he went up the seventh time to the lofty summit of Carmel and looked out towards the sea, were enabled at length to perceive the little cloud which hitherto had been small as a man's hand, expanding its volume and drawing its folds over the whole face of heaven, ready to send down in copious effusion the early and the latter rain. "Then should we grow as the lily and cast forth our roots as Lebanon. Then should our branches spread; and our beauty be as the olive tree and our smell as Lebanon. Then should they that dwell under Israel's shadow, return; they should revive as the corn and grow as the vine: the scent thereof should be as the vine of Lebanon."

It is recorded by the Spirit of God in the prophecies of Isaiah, (xi, 13,) as one of the most conspicuous marks and fruits of that glorious revival that is to usher in the final triumph of the Redeemer's kingdom, and then "the envy of Ephraim shall depart; that Ephraim shall not envy Judah, and that Judah shall not vex Ephraim." And who can doubt that the very same result would immediately follow a general revival of religion among ourselves. Under the harmonizing and subduing influences of the Spirit of God, all lesser, all merely circumstantial differences would sink and disappear, to make way for a united effort against the common enemies of Christ's cause and kingdom, and for a more sustained and strenuous exertion in extending the common salvation. Were the divine Spirit, who is a Spirit of love, to be shed abroad more abundantly in our hearts, we would think less of the small things in which we differ, and more unspeakably of the great and glorious things in which we agree. As men, when summoned forth to contest a in the dim light of the early dawn, when all things are indistinctly discerned, may often mistake and attack their friends for their foes; so where the saving light of the Spirit shines but faintly on the professing Christian world, mole-hills seem to swell into mountains, and nothing is seen in its just proportion or in the true colours which it wears. But as the rising sun absorbs the dark and chilling mists and reveals all things in the shape and form which nature gave them; so when Christ the sun of righteousness, comes forth from behind the clouds that obscured his radiant beams, and pours down by his Spirit the full blaze of His saving light upon his people, then shall they see eye to eye — and amazed and ashamed at the discovery of the trifles they had suffered so long to divide them, will be ready to say, "Come and let us walk together in the light of the Lord."

In employing this language we are very far from either insinuating, or meaning to allow, that all the points about which different denominations of true Christians disagree, are in themselves unworthy of regard. Involving, as many of them do, important Scripture principles bearing on the worship, discipline, and government of the church, they deserve the most serious consideration. But surely they are nevertheless unspeakably inferior to the grand doctrines in which all evangelical denominations are substantially at one. If they come to the same conclusion, if they have all the same answer to give to the poor perishing sinner when the great question is put, "what must I do to be saved?" there cannot surely be any very high or impassable barrier between them. And it is on this ground we feel fully warranted in expressing a strong conviction, that were there to come a time when the spirit and power of religion should be more deeply and more universally diffused; when the glory of God should become more exclusively and more prominently the grand aim of life; when the worth of immortal souls and the powers of the world to come, should be more vividly realized, Christians would stand confounded at their causes of variance, and while still formally adhering, unless new light on these points were given, to their external distinctions, would cease to make these things a cause of quarrel with each other, and become one in heart and effort in making head against infidelity and antichrist, and all the combined rulers of the darkness of this world.

A great religious revival then, would be not only an

inestimable blessing to every soul personally visited with its quickening and refreshing influence, but it would bring along with it a sure and glorious deliverance to the church of Christ. Then indeed we would need to fear no evil: for God would be in the midst of us — our God would help us, and that right early.

But there is yet an additional consideration, that should powerfully conduce to stir us up unceasingly to pray that the Lord would revive us as in the days of old. We have adverted to the present peculiar position of God's cause in these, our own lands, as seeming most urgently to require, for its preservation and prosperity, *among ourselves,* a special time of reviving and refreshing from the presence of the Lord. But let it be borne in mind, that Great Britain is manifestly at this moment the citadel of the Christian world. It has pleased God that she should long possess the faith in its greatest purity, and that she should enjoy at the same time, the most ample means for extending it throughout the earth. Her mighty colonies, and conquests, stretching from the rising to the setting sun, and giving her a commanding position in every region of the globe: her boundless commerce bringing her into immediate contact with every shore: the wealth, intelligence, and enterprise of her people, together with their prodigious advancement in all those sciences and arts which call forth the astonishment and reverence of the less enlightened nations of the earth: all these things combine to put it in the power of Britain, to bring an influence to bear on the rest of the world, unexampled perhaps in the history of mankind. Who does not see in all this a door of hope ready to open on the benighted portions of the earth; and what Christian heart that loves the Saviour and sighs over the yet limited extent of His blessed kingdom, does not beat high with the glad and glowing anticipation of the glorious outburst of saving light and health which almost seems to be at hand? Britain's Christianity and Britain's singularly favoured position together, appear in the eye of the thoughtful Christian like the streak of light which glimmers at early dawn along the horizon's verge. Let the Spirit of God give the impulse to our Christianity, causing it to spread more widely, and burn more brightly here, and we can see nothing exaggerated or over sanguine in the hope, that the light now gathering behind the mountains of Britain, shall arise like the morning sun, and pour out a flood of glory over the whole habitable earth.

But let Britain's Christianity be chilled or overborne by the many adverse influences now gathering around it, let infidelity and popery, and the liberalism of nominal Protestants, succeed in gaining the ascendancy, and the brightest ray of hope that ever opened on the world will be extinguished in darkness. It is therefore a peculiar time in which we live. It is a point in the history of God's church and of the human race, on which many converging lines at once of prophecy and of providence, seem evidently to meet. It is as when two neighbouring and hostile powers, after a long period of irregular and desultory warfare, during which neither had been making any very material or sensible impression on the other, had both at length sternly resolved to end the contest in one mighty struggle. For a time each silently prepares its means of aggression: quietly and as much as possible without attracting observation, gathering its scattered forces and training them for the conflict: labouring secretly, meanwhile, each to scatter the seeds of disaffection among the subjects of the opposing power, that when the day of decision comes, there may be not only formidable danger without, but weakness and treachery within: and when at length the mustering of armies and the frequent notes of preparation render concealment no longer practicable, the banner is openly uplifted and the trumpet of defiance blown, and then comes the dreadful onset; to end only in victory or death. There is, we say, something like this to be seen, in the present relative position of the powers of light and of darkness. For many generations, though their mutual hostility never for a moment ceased, it was carried on by means too inconsiderable and obscure to draw the attention of the world. During the last thirty years however things on both sides have been undergoing a marked and striking change. On the one side, *infidelity,* that seemed, as ashamed, to have hidden its head, has been coming again openly abroad: and popery, which appeared as if bleeding to death, or dying of old age, has suddenly exhibited symptoms of new life and energy, and has been once more opening its mouth in blasphemy and unsheathing its blood-stained sword against the saints of the Most High.

But blessed be God, on the other side too, signs at least equally decisive of growing life and vigour have contemporaneously appeared. The "good soldiers" of Jesus Christ have been finding their hands again, and putting on with renewed confidence the whole armour of God. Churches collectively, as well as private societies, of their members have been drawing together, to devise and consult for a new and more determined assault on the dominions of the wicked one. Agencies of every kind for promoting the interests of religion have been multiplying on all hands. Scriptural schools, both sabbath and week-day, for the young, additional means of religious instruction and worship for the old. Associations to circulate in all languages the holy oracles of God. Schemes of missionary enterprise to send forth the messengers of the Gospel even unto the remotest and most inaccessible quarters of the world. These and many similar indications seem manifestly to proclaim that we are on the eve of a contest of principles more tremendous that any which past ages have seen. But come when that contest may — the battle of the great day of God Almighty — we know beforehand what its issue shall be. That from the battle-field shall the triumphant shout ascend, "The kingdoms of this world are become the kingdoms of our Lord and of his Christ."

We have thus endeavoured briefly to show, both on *general* and on *special* grounds, why a revival of religion is so earnestly to be desired. We have moreover alluded to some of the encouraging circumstances which seem to warrant us in cherishing the humble hope, that the work of revival is already begun. There are still other circumstances of this kind, however, not yet noticed, though very closely connected with the republican of the instructive and admirable volume to which these remarks are prefixed, and to which therefore, in now drawing towards a conclusion, it is suitable and necessary that some reference be made. It is a striking and instructive fact that the very parish that was a chief scene of those memorable and blessed events which Mr. Robe's Narrative describes, has again, after the lapse of a hundred years, been visited with a time of peculiar reviving and refreshing from the presence of the Lord. In reading the statements concerning that parish, recently published by its present excellent minister, the Rev. Mr. Burns, we find almost an exact counterpart of the facts which the Narrative of his pious and honoured predecessor records. How true it is that even as the Lord visiteth the *iniquity* of the fathers upon the children unto the *third and fourth generation* of them that hate him, so does He show mercy unto thousands of them that *love* him and keep his comandments. As the Jews even at the time when religion had most declined among them, were beloved for their fathers' sakes, and are even now reserved for a glorious manifestation of Divine grace and love, so would it appear that the spirit of prayer which breathed throughout the parish of Kilsyth a century ago, is still telling on the welfare of its inhabitants and causing them, after a long interval of comparative deadness, to come into remembrance before God.

It is not, however, as furnishing additional materials for *theorising* on religious revivals, that we consider the reappearance of Mr. Robe's Narrative at this precise period as peculiarly important. It is for the sake of its practical uses, as a guide in seeking after and dealing with *actual* revivals of religion among ourselves that we chiefly rejoice in its being again sent abroad among Christians. There have indeed of late years been various works on this subject issuing from the press, and both the facts which they state and the increasing demand for the works themselves are the concurrent evidences of a present revival. We do not of course mean to affirm that all which is represented in these works as parktaking of that sacred character, is to be held as truly possessing it. But certainly no candid reader can examine such cases for example as those detailed in the valuable work of Dr. Sprague, without feeling abundantly satisfied that they exhibit the undoubted traces of the finger of God. At the same time no record of a religious revival occurring in a foreign country, however, interesting and instructive it may be in other respects, can possibly be so serviceable in a *practical* point of view, as the well authenticated narrative of a revival at home.

There are national peculiarities, and diversities of usage which unfit to some extent the record of the religious movements of one people, for serving as an exact rule to trace or regulate similar movements among the inhabitants of a different land. But no such disqualification attaches to the narrative of Mr. Robe. It sets before us, in the simple and familiar language of a Scottish Minister, the scenes and incidents of a Scottish revival. The lessons it conveys, therefore, bear directly upon ourselves; while they come at the same time with all the added force and attractiveness which the cherished associations of home and of country never fail to impart. We have already alluded to the similarity between the revival narrated by Mr. Robe, and the recent revival of which the parish of Kilsyth has been the scene. There is an equally close resemblance between the objections to religious revivals heard in the present day, and those which were harped upon in the times of Mr. Robe. Every one of the arguments now in the mouths of scoffers, and would-be philosophical men of the world, we find to have been as confidently and uncharitably adduced against the same work a hundred years ago, and all of them are most conclusively met and refuted by Mr. Robe and his friends. It is this very circumstance that lends so much weight and authority, which gives a character so perfectly authentic to the narrative before us. It proves that the events it records were the subject of a strict and searching investigation at the time they occurred. "The facts themselves," says Sir Henry Moncrieff in his Life of Dr. Erskine, "whatever view may be taken of them, are ascertained by the most unquestionable evidence, by the testimony of Mr. John Maclaurin of Glasgow, who was most assiduous and minute in his investigation of them,* by Dr. John Hamilton of the High Church of Glasgow, whose good sense and discernment were worthy of the high respectability of his character,† by Mr. Robe of Kilsyth, whose integrity was never questioned, and who published a narrative on the subject,‡ Dr. Webster of Edinburgh, who accompanied Mr. Whitefield and preached with him at Cambuslang: who published an account of what he represented as real conversions there, in opposition to those who pronounced them a delusion, who wrote from his personal knowledge and attested the facts of which he was an eye-witness,§ and by Dr. Erskine himself, who was then a student in divinity, and who wrote a pamphlet on the subject†, entitled "The Signs of the Times"; and after reviewing the attempts which in opposition to these various writers, were made by others who were unfriendly, to bring odium on the revival of that period, or to explain it away, by ascribing it to mere physical excitement or wild fanaticism, Sir Henry pronouces this temperate and well merited rebuke on the authors of these unworthy efforts to discredit or disparage the work of the Spirit of God: a rebuke not inapplicable to some in the present day.

"Whatever opinion, says he, may be held with respect to the means or influence with which four hundred individuals connected a reformation in their moral and religious character, which they afterwards supported through life, no fair man will deny, that such an effect,

* Account of his life, prefixed to his Sermons and Essays.
† In his letters to Mr. Prince of Boston, 1742, published in the Life of Whitefield.
‡ The Narrative now reprinted.
§ Webster's "Divine Influence, the true spring of the extraordinary work at Cambuslang." And his second edition of ditto, with a preface, in answer to Mr. Fisher's Review.

produced in such a number of human beings, is a subject neither of ridicule nor contempt. Many thousands attended on whom no visible impression seems to have been made. And this fact, according with ordinary experience, and honestly related in the narrative on the subject, confirms instead of lessening their credibility.

"On the other hand, let the thousands who go away without having received any visible impression be out of the question, (though many good effects might have been produced which were neither observed nor related at the time) four hundred individuals who to the conviction of those who knew them, became better men, men more useful and conscientious in their stations and more faithful in their practical duties than they ever were before, and who preserve this character while they live: exhibits a view of the religion of Cambuslang and Kilsyth, which a wise man will not easily bring himself to reprobate: and which no good man, if he candidly examines the facts, and believes them, will allow himself to despise."

This one testimony, from such a man as the biographer of Erskine, prëeminently distinguished as he was both for the strength and the soundness of his mind, will, in the estimation of every intelligent Christian, far more than outweight all the rash assertions or injurious misrepresentations of mere men of the world. It was remarked near the beginning of this Essay, as a strange thing that the word *revival* should sound so offensively when used in connection with religion, to multitudes who, in any other connection, are ready to hail it as bringing every glad and grateful association in its train. It *is* strange, undoubtedly, and as we have endeavoured to show, when the subject is considered in relation to its own proper and intrinsic merits: but it is *not* strange

when viewed with reference to the fallen and corrupt nature of man. The gospel itself is an offence to the unregenerate mind, and for the very same reason, so is a religious revival. Formal professors of Christianity, who have accustomed themselves to consider religion as requiring little more than certain decent external observances, are naturally alarmed and irritated when they find it forcing itself, by some great and simultaneous movement of a whole community, into close and immediate contact with the whole current and business of life. They could not only endure it, but even willingly pay to it all outward respect and deference, so long as it could be kept at arm's length. But when a whole neighbourhood is seen to be commoved upon the subject, when the concerns of the soul, and of the world to come, are found engrossing men's minds, mingling in their daily conversation, and coming forth with all that power and prominence which rightly belong to the "one thing needful," the impulse such an event gives to public feeling overbears and breaks down those fences with which unspiritual men had been keeping religion at a distance from them. They cannot in such a state of things get rid of it, go where they will. They are left with no choice but either to maintain that the subjects of that revival have a great deal too much of religion, or that they themselves have a great, great deal too little. But this painful sensation among worldly men, which a religious revival creates, is not therefore to be regarded as an evil: on the contrary, it is to be considered as one of the most important blessings such a revival involves. It is like a spring breaking out under a stagnant pool, sending up by the first rush of its waters the mud which had lain quietly at the bottom, but destined by its continued flow to purify and sweeten that which before had been only the parent of corruption.   ROBERT BUCHAN
Dec. 15th, 1839.   *Minister of Tron Church, Glasgow.*

PREFACE

IT is transporting and astonishing, that after all the great and horrid provocations we have given the Most High in this church and land, by growing deism and infidelity, carnality and profanity, formality and hypocrisy, our bitter envyings and unreasonable divisions, but most of all by a general rejecting of the blessed Son of God by unbelief, and using gospel ordinances contentedly without feeling the power of them, the Lord hath been so far from utterly forsaking us, and making our country desolate by some destroying judgment, that he is in "wrath remembering mercy," and beginning manifestly to revive his work, and help us in such a situation as was become hopeless and helpless by any human possible means.

There hath been a great and just complaint among godly ministers and Christians of the elder sort, who have seen better days, that for some years past there hath been a sensible decay as to the life and power of godliness. "Iniquity abounded and the love of many waxed cold." Our defection from the Lord, and backsliding, increased fast to a dreadful apostasy. While the government, worship, and doctrine established in this church were retained in profession; there hath been a universal corruption of life, reaching even unto the sons and daughters of God. Former strictness as to holiness and tenderness of life was much relaxed among both ministers and people of the better sort: a formal round of professional duties was the religion of the professors, and in this they rested: as to the multitude they were visibly profane, and without any sense of religion at all. Things were become so bad with us, that there were few that we, the ministers of the word, could comfort as believers in Christ, and exhort to rejoice in hope of the glory of God, when we found them adying. All this was observed by some, and looked upon as the cause of God's controversy with us; and what, they feared, would provoke him to send some desolating judgment, to avenge the quarrel of his thus broken covenant: and in this view they gave warning as occasion offered.

It is one of Satan's devices, to engage some distressed souls, to be deeply exercised about things which either are not their sins, or among the least of them; that thereby he may divert them from minding their greatest sins, and those which are the cause of God's controversy with them. Some zealous good men, both ministers and others, fell unwarily into this snare. They looked upon some things of mismanagement in government and discipline, which others were dissastified with as well as they, with such earnestness, that they cried out against them as the most crying sins, the cause of the Lord's controversy with us, portending dreadful judgments, and what corrupted the church so far that nothing could secure the salvation of her members but coming out of her and separating from her. Hereby they were led to overlook what was our greatest evil, and the cause of God's controversy with us, namely, the corruption of the lives of the members of this church, and that we had a name to live, while we were in a great measure dead as to faith, love to God and one another, and other branches of holiness.

This unhappily filled the heads and mouths of most professors to such a degree, as to mind and converse about nothing even upon the Lord's day but ministers, church judicatories, and some other disputable things, far from the vitals of religion. The state of their souls was much forgotten, and they were either disaffected to their worthy ministers, and the Lord's ordinances dispensed by them; or if they attended, they were diverted by these things from a concern about their regeneration, conversion, and amending their ways and doings which were not good. Wherever our lamentable divisions prevailed, serious religion declined to a shadow.

All this while we had a dead and barren time. The work of conversion went but slowly and undiscernibly on. The influences of the Holy Spirit were restrained. The Lord's presence was much withdrawn, and the power of his grace but little exerted and put forth, so that the gospel had but small success, either for bringing souls to Jesus Christ, or for quickening and refreshing real Christians. Ministers and godly Christians, who observed these things with sorrow, were filled with tears lest the Lord had poured forth a spirit of deep sleep upon this generation, and given unto his servants the commission he gave unto the evangelical prophet Isaiah: "And he said, Go, and tell this people, Hear ye indeed, but understand not; and see ye indeed, but perceive not. Make the heart of this people fat, and make their ears heavy, and shut their eyes: lest they see with their eyes, and hear with their ears, and understand with their heart, and convert and be healed. Then said I, Lord, how long? and he answered, Untill the cities be wasted without inhabitant, and the houses without man, and the land be utterly desolate, and the Lord have removed men far away, and there be a great forsaking in the midst of the land." Several ministers gave warning to their people, that they were afraid lest these spiritual judgments most frequent in the New Testament times were inflicted upon many of them, and might be still further.

Things being come to this extremity, it was the Lord's opportunity to glorify his name in a way surprising to us, and peculiar to himself. We were going on towardly in the way of our heart, notwithstanding a variety of smiting judgments and alluring mercies: He, in his sovereign mercy and goodness, hath begun to see our ways and to heal them, when we were proof against all other dispensations; he hath visited us with such a dispensation of his Spirit as is sufficient to do it, and we pray that it may and hope that it shall be general unto the whole church and land. This extraordinary out-pouring of the Holy Spirit, whereby great numbers of secure sinners are awakened, and many of them converted and filled with faith and more than ordinary peace and joy in believing, appeared first upon the 18th of February last, and continues at Cambuslang, a parish within four miles south-east of Glasgow. A well attested Narrative of this hath been published.

Blessed be the God and Father of our Lord Jesus Christ, that this sensible presence and power of the Holy Ghost hath not been confined to that highly favoured parish, but began to visit us upon Sabbath the 25th day of April last, as it soon after did also several other congregations lying to the north, north-east, and north-west of Glasgow. This work so extraordinary upon the souls of many in these congregations is the same with that at Cambuslang. The method of the Spirit's operation is alike in all these congregations; and the effects of it upon the bodies of the awakened, which have not been

33

so common at other times, are also much the same.

The bodies of some of the awakened are seized with trembling, fainting, hysteries in some few women, and with convulsive motions in some others, arising from that apprehension and fear of the wrath of God they are convinced they are under and liable to because of their sins. They have a quick apprehension of the greatness and dreadfulness of this wrath before they are affected.

These effects upon the bodies of some of the awakened have been objected against this work by many. And some have not been afraid to ascribe it to the Devil, and to traduce the whole as delusion.

As there were the very same appearances accompanying such an effusion of the Holy Spirit in some of our American colonies; so the same objections were made against them which have been made against this appearance of God among us. This hath occasioned the reverend and judicious Mr. Edwards, minister of the gospel at Northampton in New England, to preach and publish a sermon upon the distinguishing marks of a work of the Spirit of God, wherein he answers and takes off the foresaid objections in a satisfactory manner. It would be superfluous and unnecessary again to answer these objections after him, seeing this sermon hath been oftener than once reprinted in North Britain, and is and will be in as many hands as any other answer probably can, with this advantage, that by the surprising direction of Providence it comes from one in a foreign country, who preached and published it long before this appearance of the Lord in his glory and majesty amongst us.

The judgment and desire of friends which I value have had considerable weight with me to essay the following Narrative, with a dependence upon the Divine assistance, and as the Lord shall permit. The omission of our worthy forefathers to transmit to posterity a full and circumstantial account of the conversion of five hundred by one sermon at the kirk of Shotts in the year 1630 — of the beginning and progress of the extraordinary outletting of the Holy Spirit in the west of Scotland already mentioned, I have heard much complained of and lamented. And I cannot but think that if after such complaints we are guilty of the same neglect we will be more blame-worthy before God, our own consciences, and posterity.

But that which most of all prevails with me is, that as I, in the most express and deliberate manner I can, design and intend it to the praise and glory of God, renouncing all other ends contrary to this; so I am persuaded it will by his blessing contribute to it.

Every godly one into whose hands it may come will doubtless find matter of praise from it to the Lord. Others who laboured under mistakes anent this work, through prejudices from opinions they have entertained as to the manner wherein the Lord might come to revive his work in this church, may possibly, when they hear these things, hold their peace, and glorify God, saying. Then hath God also granted repentance unto life unto our brethren whom we hated; as the apostles and church of Jerusalem did when they heard of the conversion of the despised Gentiles. And doubtless others, when they hear of the Lord's bringing so many of Zion's prisoners "out of the fearful pit and miry clay," and putting a new song in their mouth, even praise to our God, shall by his grace be brought to fear and trust in the Lord.

But praise to our God, for these his mighty acts are not to be confined to the present generation, wherein they appear. Posterity shall reap the benefit of them, and it is our duty to transmit the history of them to posterity, that they may reap the greater benefit by them, and praise the Lord more distinctly for them. It would be a contempt of these wonderful works which God hath made to be had in remembrance, if they should be buried in oblivion, so as not to be known by those who live in after ages. One generation should praise his works to another, and should declare his mighty acts. This we are expressly commanded to do, that after generations may put their trust in God and praise him. "This shall be written for the generation to come, and the people which shall be created shall praise the Lord." "For he established a testimony in Jacob, and appointed a law in Israel, which he commanded our fathers, that they should make them known to their children. That the generation to come might know them, even the children which should be born: who should arise and declare them to their children: that they might set their hope in God, and not forget the works of God."

In this Narrative I propose to give an account of this surprising dispensation of grace, in the beginning, progress, and various circumstances of it, with the strictest regard to truth in all the exactness I can. A polished style is not to be expected from one who must redeem time from eating and sleeping to carry it on. To write intelligibly is all I aim at. I have no view of leisure to publish above a sheet of it once a week or fortnight; and this is the reason why it is not emitted at once. To serve the truth and the interests of religion, and to satisfy the longing curiosity of those who are giving Zion's King no rest untill he make his Jerusalem a praise in the midst of the earth, are what I intended.

May the Holy Spirit, whose work upon the souls of many is to be narrated, accompany the Narrative with his powerful influences, that it may promote the Redeemer's interest, and make every reader feel, by his saving operations, that he is indeed come in an uncommon way of grace. Any may this whole church and all the ends of the earth see greater things than these.   Amen.

JAMES ROBE.

KILSYTH, July 29th, 1742.

Chapter 1

Revival at Kilsyth

THE town and parish of Kilsyth, formerly and ordinarily, untill of late, called Moniabroch, are situate between the river Kelvin and the river Carron, and in the shire of Stirling.

The people of the said parish, above eleven hundred examinable persons, are, for the most part, of a discreet and towardly disposition. I was settled among them in the year 1713; they have lived peaceably with and carried themselves dutifully towards me. The most part of them have attended upon public ordinances and means of instruction as well as any about them. The most of them, who are about or under forty years, have attained such a measure of knowledge of the principles of religion as renders them inferior to few of their station and education.

For several years they appeared to profit under gospel ordinances, by the blessing of the Lord upon them. In December, 1732, and January. 1733, the Lord visited us with a distressing calamity and heavy judgments. There were many of the elder sort carried off by a pleuretic fever after a few days' illness. Upwards of sixty were in the space of three weeks buried in the church-yard. What made this dispensation more threatening was that the most religious and judicious Christians in this congregation were removed from us thereby. This made me fear some dreadful evil to come upon the surviving generation. I publish to the praise and glory of God, and with thankful acknowledgements to his mercy and power, that I enjoyed then a state of health and strength uncommon to me, as I do at this time, though I travelled from morning till late at night, all the days of the week, among the sick and dying.

After this the state of religion declined, and grew every year worse with us. Our societies for prayer came gradually to nothing. The younger sort attained indeed to knowledge, took up a profession, and numbers of them were yearly added to the communicants: but I could observe little of the power of godliness in their lives that was satisfying to me. As to the elder sort, those of them who were graceless and Christless went on in their former sins and carelessness, without any appearance of a change to the better: those who were professors seemed sensibly to degenerate into a negligence and indifference about spiritual things, and some of them into drunkenness and other vices.

Upon the 27th of June, 1733, about and after mid-day, being Wednesday, there was such a dreadful storm of thunder, hail, and rain, as no man living had ever seen. The fire burnt a woman and child, but both their lives were preserved, while a cat was killed at one of her feet, and a pitcher, with some other things, were broken to pieces at the other. The hail was incredibly large, some of it, which I measured myself, being three inches round. It destroyed much of the corn to the east of the town of Kilsyth. The floods came from the mountains so great and rapid that they carried down stones a great way into the plain lying beneath the town of Kilsyth, and these of prodigious bigness. There were above a thousand cart loads of them, and many two or three yards in depth and thickness. Some houses were carried away, a good number of cattle drowned, and the most of the corn in the low grounds destroyed. The loss of the parish was moderately computed at a thousand pounds sterling. Yet I could not observe any one person amended by it, or seeking to the Lord for all this.

When our unhappy divisions broke out, only about ten or twelve deserted my ministry. They were of no consideration as to serious religion, or even knowledge, except one, who some time since saw his error and returned. Yet though the body of the people were not carried away by this evil, they were so bewitched as to decline to the separating side, and were so taken up with disputable things, that little concern about those of the greatest importance could be observed among them. All the societies for prayer were then given up. I gave fair and open warning, from the first appearance of the division, against it. I continually instructed them in the evil and dreadful consequences of it. Though such warnings were not well relished by many, yet I am persuaded the Lord blessed them, to preserve the body of the congregation out of those dangerous paths; and I know several of them are now sensible of God's mercy and goodness to them in this. By the power of God accompanying his ordinances, life was kept in the few who were made alive to God, through Jesus Christ; and others had knowledge begun and increased, as a foundation laid beforehand for this work of the Holy Spirit.

Under the late dearth this people suffered greatly; the poor were numerous, and many, especially about the town of Kilsyth, were at the point of starving: yet, as I frequently observed to them, I could not see any one turning to the Lord who smote them, or crying to him because of their sins, while they howled upon their beds for bread. Instead of this, theft and other immoralities

40

brake forth and increased to a terrible height. The return of plenty had no better influence upon us; but we were going on forwardly, in the way of our own heart, when the Lord came to see our ways and heal them, by this uncommon dispensation of his grace; all this hath been narrated, that every one may observe the sovereign freedom and riches of grace in visiting after this sort so sinful, degenerate, and ungainable a people. Surely not for our sakes but for his own holy name's sake he hath done it, that we may now be ashamed and confounded for our evil ways.

In the year 1740 I began to preach upon the doctrine of regeneration. The method I followed, by the Divine direction, was first to press the importance and necessity of it, which I did from John, iii, 3: "Except a man be born again, he cannot see the kingdom of God." Next I showed the mysteriousness of the way and manner of the Holy Spirit in effecting it, from John, iii, 8: "The wind bloweth where it listeth, and thou hearest the sound thereof, but canst not tell whence it cometh and whither it goeth: so is every one that is born of the Spirit." I proceeded, thirdly, to explain and apply the various Scripture views and expressions of it: as first, Being born again, from the forequoted John, iii, 8. Secondly, A resurrection, from Rev. xx, 6: "Blessed and holy is he that hath part in the first resurrection." Thirdly, A new creation, from Eph. ii, 10: "For we are his workmanship, created in Jesus Christ unto good works." Fourthly, Christ's conquest of the sinner to himself, from Psal. cx, 3: "Thy people shall be willing in the day of thy power." Fifthly, The circumcision of the heart, from Ezek. xliv, 9: "Thus saith the Lord God, No stranger uncircumcised in heart, nor uncircumcised in flesh, shall enter into my sanctuary, of any stranger among the children of Israel." This was also intended to show the necessity of regeneration, in order to the receiving the Lord's supper worthily, to be dispensed in the congregation about that time. Here this subject was interrupted untill the end of last year; when I, resuming it, preached regeneration as it is. Sixthly, The taking away the stony heart, and the giving the heart of flesh, from Ezek. xi, 19. Seventhly, The putting of God's law in the mind, and writing it in the heart, from Heb. viii, 10.

I sometimes could observe that the doctrine of these sermons was acceptable to the Lord's people, and that there was more than ordinary seriousness in hearing them, yet could see no further fruit. But now I find that the Lord, who is infinitely wise, and knoweth the end from the beginning, was preparing some for this uncommon dispensation of the Spirit that we looked not for; and that others were brought under convictions issuing, by the power of the Highest, in their real conversion, and in a silent way.

When the news were first brought me of the extraordinary outpouring of the Holy Ghost at Cambuslang, I rejoiced at them. I prayed continually for the continuance of it there, and that the Lord would thus visit us in these bounds, and spake of it sometimes to the congregation, which was not without some good fruits, as I have learned since: Particularly, I was informed by the minister of Cambuslang, and another reverend and very dear brother, that a young man from the parish of Falkirk, who had been awakened at Cambuslang, and was in a hopeful condition, said, that the occasion of his coming there was his hearing me, the Sabbath immediately preceding, praise the appearance of the Lord at the aforesaid place, and that this strongly inclined him to go thither.

There were few of the people under my charge went to Cambuslang, notwithstanding of what they heard me say

42

of it. Some of the better sort went once or twice: but I scarcely heard of any who needed most of the work of the Comforter to convince them of sin, righteousness, and of judgment, that went there untill the 13th of May, when there were a good many, but came all away, as far as I knew them, without any deep or lasting impressions upon them. It was matter of discouragement to me when I heard that my brethren in Cumbernauld, Kirkintilloch, Calder, and Campsie, had several persons in their parishes awakened at Cambuslang, and that I had not one so much as the least touched to my knowledge. What appeared the most hopeful was that there appeared a concern more than ordinary among the hearers of the gospel, and that there were proposals for setting up societies for prayer, which had been long intermitted.

Upon Thursday evening, the 15th of April last, Mr. John Willison, minister of the gospel at Dundee, came to my house in his return from Cambuslang, whither he had gone the Saturday before. I desired him to preach to us upon the Friday morning, which he readily complied with: a great multitude of people met, though the warning was very short. He preached a distinct, plain, and moving sermon, from Psalm xl, 2, 3: "He brought me up also out of a horrible pit, out of the miry clay, and set my feet upon a rock, and established my goings: and he hath put a new song in my mouth, even praise to our God. Many shall see it and fear, and shall trust in the Lord." Several of those now awakened date their first serious concern about their souls from their hearing this sermon, and the blessing of the Lord upon it.

The following Sabbath I entered upon the view of regeneration as it is expressed Gal. iv, 19: "My little children, of whom I travail in birth again untill Christ be formed in you." I had more than ordinary tenderness in reading of that text, and could scarcely do it without tears and emotion. I observed much seriousness among the hearers.

The last Sabbath and 25th day of April, one woman was awakened in this congregation to a very distressing sight of her sin and danger thereby. She lived in the parish of Campsie. She was observed by some to be under great uneasiness in the congregation, but made no outcry; she went away when the congregation was dismissed, but was not able to go far; she was found soon in a field in great distress, and crying out, what would she do to be saved; she was brought back to me, and I conversed with her all that evening, in the presence of several judicious persons. She fainted once or twice. I observed every thing narrowly and exactly about her, because it was a new thing to me, and I knew the objections made against the work at Cambuslang. She seemed to be a healthy woman, and about twenty years of age; she said, that in hearing the sermon she was made to see that she was unlike Jesus Christ, and like the devil, and in a state of unregeneracy. She had strong impressions of the greatness of the wrath of God she was lying under and liable to. She went away composed and calm, in a hopeful condition. She continued many weeks now and then much distressed; but hath some time ago attained, through grace, to sensible relief, and by the testimony of the neighbourhood, her conversation is such as becometh the gospel.

About this time sixteen children, or thereby, in the town of Kirkintilloch, were observed to meet together in a barn for prayer; the occasion of which was, that one of them said to the rest, What need is there that we should always play, had we not better go and pray? wherewith the rest complied. The Rev. Mr. Burnside, as soon as he heard of it, carefully enquired after them, and met frequently with them, for their direction and instruction. And, as I am informed, they make progress and continue in a hopeful way. This made much noise in the country-side, and deep impressions both upon young and old.

This week I visited the families of a part of this parish, where I observed more than ordinary seriousness amongst the people, and more than ordinary liberty, freedom, and earnestness in my dealing with them. It was matter of trouble and exercise to me, however, that none under my charge that I knew of were awakened, and I was much in my way of thinking like several of those now awakened, who were concerned at first lest the Lord had passed them by when he was awakening others. Such were my fears about this parish.

Nothing appeared more than ordinary upon the first Sabbath of May. Near this time, and a little before, there were some societies for prayer formed in the parish; I was also informed, that several young girls in the town of Kilsyth, from ten to sixteen years of age, had been observed meeting together for prayer in an out-house they had access to.

May 9th, being the second Lord's day that month, four or five were awakened to a distressing sight of their sinful and lost estate, though only two of them were known to me upon the said day. I prayed and hoped that this might be like some drops before a plentiful rain.

May 11th, There was a great and a good day of the Son of man at Auchenloch in the parish of Calder. The Rev. Mr. Warden, their minister, preached at that place. There was a great cry in that congregation, and about fourteen brought under great concern and anxiety about their spiritual and eternal state.

May 12th. I went to Cambuslang and preached there, as did also some other ministers, upon the next day. I was witness there to a great day of the Mediator's power, and learned much that by the Lord's blessing hath been useful to me in assisting the Lord's people brought under spiritual distress here.

May 14th, being Friday, I left Cambuslang in the morning. I met an event in my way homeward which much surprised me, and I could not but observe the Lord's hand remarkably in it. I promised to meet a friend at a gentleman's house betwixt Cambuslang and Kilsyth upon the Tuesday evening, but could not leave Cambuslang that night. I purposed therefore to be early at the said gentleman's house next day. Though the road by which I went to Cambuslang was unexceptionably good, I was strongly inclined to try a much nearer way, altogether unknown to me, notwithstanding some dissuaded me from it because of mosses and other inconveniences. In my way I came to a house which I was told belonged to Messrs. Gray, and that their bleachfield was there. I remembered that these gentlemen were married to the daughters of a gentleman whom I knew and highly esteemed from my youth, and since I found myself at their gate, I enquired for them, with a purpose not to alight. One of the gentlemen and his lady were at home: they urged me to come into their house, though it should be only for a little, which I did. They told me that six of their servants had been awakened at Cambuslang some days since, and desired me to converse with them. I had such a strong inclination to get forward in my journey that I declined it: they desired me to pray in their family, which I cheerfully complied with. After prayer I spoke a few words, as the Lord helped me, to their numerous servants who were present, relating to the case of those who were under soul-distressing convictions of their sin and danger, as also of those who never had been under them. Having dismissed them, I went to take my horse.

Ere I got to him, a noise was heard among the servants, and we were told that one of them was fallen into great uneasiness and was crying bitterly. I returned to the house and she was brought to me. I had conversed but a very short time with her, when a second was brought to me, then a third, in a little after that two together, last of all a sixth, crying out for their lost and undone state, and what should they do. I prayed and conversed with them for some time. I was much moved with this providence. "The Lord who leads the blind in a way that they know not," led me to this house without any thought or purpose of mind; yea contrary to my inclination, which was to hasten forward. He managed my aversion (which I now see to have been sinful,) to converse with the first six under distress, to bring about his own holy and glorious ends: for if I had conversed with them, I had not seen the other servants. His ways are a great deep. Mr. Whitefield, when I told him this story, said, "Only he must needs go through Samaria." I was greatly pleased to observe the Christian affectionate and zealous care Mr. and Mrs. Gray had for their distressed servants.

May 16th I preached, as I had done for some time past, from Gal. iv, 29. In the forenoon I insisted upon a use of consolation, and in the afternoon pressed all the unregenerate to seek to have Christ formed in them. An extraordinary power of the Spirit from on high accompanied the word preached. There was a great mourning in the congregation, as for an only son. Many cried out; and these not only women, but some strong and stout-hearted young men, and some betwixt forty and fifty.

After the dismission of the congregation, an attempt was made to get the distressed into my barn, but it could not be done. The number of them and of their friends attending them were so many, I was obliged to convene them in the kirk. I sung a psalm and prayed with them;

but when I attempted to speak to them I could not be heard, such were their bitter cries and groans, and the voice of their weeping.

After this I ordered that they should be brought to me in my closet one by one. I sent also for the Rev. Mr. Oughterson, minister of Cumbernauld, to assist me in dealing with the distressed that evening, who readily came. In the mean time I appointed psalms to be sung with those in the kirk, and that the precentor, with two or three of the elders, should pray with the distressed; which the extraordinariness of this event seemed to me to warrant. At the same time I forbade any to exhort or speak to them in the congregation, that I might cut off occasion of calummy and objection from those who seemed to desire it.

The noise of the distressed was so great that it was heard from afar. It was pleasant to hear those who were in a state of enmity with God, despisers of Jesus Christ, and Satan's contented slaves, some of them crying out for mercy, some that they were lost and undone, others. "What shall we do to be saved? others praising God for this day, and for awakening them; and others not only weeping and crying for themselves, but for their graceless relatives. And yet it would have moved the hardest heart that, as the children of Israel under Pharaoh's oppression, when I spake unto many of them they hearkened not for anguish of spirit and the sense of the cruel bondage they were under.

There appeared about thirty awakened this day, belonging to this and the neighbouring congregations. About twenty of them belonged to this parish. Some few to the parish of Campsie, and the remainder to that of Kirkintilloch. But I have found since, in conversing with the distressed, and that the number of the awakened far exceeds thirty.

Wednesday, 19th, We had sermon for the first time upon a week-day. I preached, as did also the Rev. Mr. Warden, minister of Campsie, and the Rev. Mr. M'Laurin, Glasgow, who had come hither the night before upon my invitation. The number of the awakened this day were as many as were upon the Lord's day. The greatest number was from the parish of Kirkintilloch: there were also some from the parishes of Campsie and Cumbernauld. The number of the awakened belonging to this parish amounted this week to forty.

May 20th, The minister of Kirkintilloch, Mr. M'Laurin, and I, preached at Kirkintilloch. There we saw Zion's mighty King appearing in his glory and majesty, and his arrows sharp in the heart of his enemies. Many were awakened there and brought under great spiritual distress.

Having brought this Narrative to the first considerable and remarkable outpouring of the Holy Spirit upon this corner, before I proceed to the intended method of this Narrative, it will no doubt be satisfying to my readers to know the progress this blessed work hath made, and the number of the awakened in the several parishes into which, by the Lord's mercy, it hath entered, as far as I am informed, or upon some good grounds can guess.

There have been at least three hundred awakened in this parish since the beginning of this work, of which about two hundred belong or did belong to this parish. There were indeed about fourteen or fifteen of them awakened when Mr. Whitefield preached at Cumbernauld. In the parish of Cumbernauld there are above eighty.

In the parish of Kirkintilloch there are known to the minister about a hundred and twenty under a more than ordinary concern about their salvation, including the praying young, who are increased now to a greater number than formerly mentioned.

In the parish of St. Ninians, the number of the awakened must be considerable. The first remarkable appearance of this good work there was at the giving the holy supper, upon the first of this current August. There were several awakened upon the Saturday, many more upon the Lord's day, both in the kirk, during the action sermon and the service, and also in the congregation in the fields. There were yet a far greater number upon the Monday, which was one of the greatest days of the Mediator's power I have hitherto seen. Many of the awakened belong to that parish, as also to the parish of Gargunnock. By a letter from the Rev. Mr. Mackie, minister of that parish, I am informed, that the number of the awakened was increased upon the Thursday thereafter, when they had sermon. He appoints days for them to come to him for instruction and direction.

In the parish of Gargunnock, lying west from the parish of St. Ninians, there are, as I am well informed, nearly a hundred persons awakened. There were some of them first of all awakened at Kilsyth, when the Lord's Supper was given, upon the second Sabbath of July; others at Campsie, when it was given upon the last Sabbath of the same month; others at St. Ninians, when that sacrament was given upon the first Sabbath of August. Upon the Thursday thereafter, there were eighteen awakened in their own congregation, while the Rev. Mr. Warden, their own aged and diligent pastor, preached to them. There was also a considerable awakening the week thereafter, the son of the minister of Campsie preaching there. The minister of this parish hath always had a singular dexterity in instructing and dealing with the consciences of the people under his charge, and it is to be hoped that there will be a good account of the awakened in that congregation, by the

Lord's blessing upon the skill and will he hath given to his servant to win them to Jesus Christ.

In the parish of Calder, according to the information I have from their minister, there are above a hundred awakened.

There are about the same number in the parish of Campsie.

The case of the parish of Baldernock, lying north-west from Calder, is of all others the most singular and noticeable. There were above ninety awakened persons in that parish about the sixth of July last. They have been for some years past and yet are without a pastor. Their late pastor, Mr. Robert Wallace, who deceased among them, had the charge of their souls above fifty years: he was pious, faithful, diligent, and dearly beloved by his people; and, as I am informed, there was no person among them was carried away by the Secession. The Lord hath honoured their schoolmaster, James Forsyth, to be greatly instrumental in this good work among them. I shall give the following extract from a letter of his, dated Baldernock, July 17th, 1742, concerning the impressions made upon and the awakening of several of the young ones: he writes, "Since the first of February last, I endeavoured to instruct the children under my charge, to the utmost of my power, in the first principles of religion — that they were born in a state of sin and misery, and strangers to God by nature. I also pressed them by all arguments possible, to leave off their sinful ways, and fly to Jesus Christ by faith and repentance; which, by the blessing of God, hath not been in vain. Glory to his holy name, that backed with the power of his Holy Spirit what was spoken in much weakness. I likewise warned them against the commission of any known sin, and told them their danger if they persisted in the same, and that their sins would find them out. These

51

exhortations frequently repeated, yea almost every day, came at last to have some impression on their young hearts. And I think the great concern that was at first among them was a mean in God's hand to bring the elder sort to a more serious concern, and to more diligence in religious duties; yea, I heard some say, that they were ashamed to hear and see these young creatures so much taken up about their souls' salvation. That is some account of the rise of this good and happy work. There was one of the schoolboys that went to Cambuslang in March that was first awakened; he, after some few days, said to me, in the school, will you let two or three of us meet together to sing psalms and pray? I said, I was very well pleased to hear that they were inclined to such a good exercise; so they joined themselves together, and it hath had very good fruit. For some few days after there were some of them under concern, and that day fourteen days after they first met there were ten or twelve awakened and under deep convictions, some very young, of eight and nine years of age, some twelve and thirteen. They still inclined more and more to their duty, so that they meet three times a day — in the morning, at night, and at noon. Also they have forsaken all their childish fancies and plays; so those that have been awakened are known by their countenance and conversation, their walk and behaviour. The work among the young ones in the school still increases, and there are still some newly awakened. There were some that by a word of terror in their lesson were very distressed, and would cry out and weep bitterly. There are some of them very sensible of their case, both the sin of their nature and their actual transgressions, and even of the sin of unbelief; for when I would exhort any of them that were distressed, to believe in Christ, because he is both able and willing to save to the uttermost, they replied, that they knew he was both able and willing; but they could not believe themselves, unless God gave them a heart so to do; for, they said, they felt their heart so hard that they could do nothing." Such is the account he gives of the younger sort. "As to the elder sort," he says, "the first among them were awakened at Cambuslang, others at Calder and Kirkintilloch; but the greatest part have been awakened at their society meetings. They meet twice a week for prayer and praise, where all the awakened in the parish, with as many others as please to come, are admitted." There are also several other little meetings, almost every day, in different places of the parish. At the second of these meetings there were nine awakened, at the third there were four, at another meeting there were five or six. He says that there is a greater diligence about the concerns of religion, even among the careless and ignorant, than ever was known before, and that the younger sort are so taken up with religion that they esteem it more than their necessary food. There are several under deep conviction who were formerly rude and profane. In another letter, dated July 6th, 1742, he says, that this good work still continues among them, and that there are a considerable number newly awakened in the parish besides strangers that come to their meetings from other parishes. There were two young women in a neighbouring parish who had been at Cambuslang and brought back an evil report of what they had been witness to there; they said they wondered what made the people cry out. Upon the 22nd of June they came to one of these meetings in Baldernock, as was supposed, with no good design; they had not been above three quarters of an hour in the meeting when they were brought under convictions and continued in distress the whole time the meeting lasted. He says there are a goodly number of them who have found relief, which seems to be real from scripture marks and evidences they give of it.

I have been more particular in this article concerning Baldernock,[1] that we who are ministers of the gospel may learn from this, not to be lifted up from any success we may have in our ministrations; seeing that though the Lord maketh especially the preaching of the word an effectual mean of convincing and converting sinners, and of building up them that are converted, yet he also blesseth the reading of the word, Christian communion, and religious education, by parents, schoolmasters, and others, for the foresaid blessed ends: and that he can and sometimes doth make use of weak and inconsiderable instruments for beginning and carrying on a good work upon the souls of men, while men of great gifts and even godliness are not so successful. This is the more to be regarded as the doing of the Lord, that the people of Baldernock are not the less careful to attend upon public ordinances, neither is their esteem of them diminished. Their meetings do not interfere with the dispensation of public ordinances in their own congregation when they have it, nor with that in the neighbouring congregations when they want it in their own. It is also hoped that the reading of the foresaid article may excite schoolmasters and others who have the education of youth, to be diligent in instructing the youngest of them in the principles of our holy religion, and to endeavour daily to make impressions upon their tender minds, of their sinful and lost state by nature, and of their only remedy by Jesus Christ.

In the parish of Killearn, lying about seven miles to the north-west of Campsie, this good work is also begun. The Rev. Mr. Bain hath been well affected to it from the beginning, and was early witness to it and assisting to

[1]August 25th, the awakened there are now about a hundred.

54

carry it on at Cambuslang. There was a considerable awakening in this parish when the Lord's Supper was given there, upon the third Sabbath of July, especially upon the Monday, when the Rev. Mr. Potter, professor of divinity in the university of Glasgow, and the Rev. Mackie, minister of St. Ninians, preached.

In the country west from Glasgow there are very joyful accounts of the entrance and progress of this blessed work there. In the town of Irvine there were a few awakened first at Cambuslang, but now there are a good many awakened that never were at Cambuslang, and are in very great distress and anguish of soul, like those at Cambuslang and in this country. They are happy under the inspection and care of their worthy minister, Mr. M'Kneight. In the parish of Long Dreghorn, and other parishes about, there are several awakened. In the town of Kilmarnock there were about fifty from that place awakened at Cambuslang, but there have been many more since in their own congregations. This blessed work hath made less progress to the eastward of Kilsyth, the people being much distracted and divided by the influence of the Seceders, and even furiously prejudiced against the dispensation of ordinances in this church, yet, blessed be the Lord, it extends even to these congregations. In the parish of Denny there are several, some of whom have been awakened in their own church. There are several in the united parishes of Dunnipace and Larbert, some of whom have been awakened likewise there. In the parish of Torphichen, south from Linlithgow, there were seven awakened, when the Lord's Supper was given there, upon the first Sabbath of August.

Though I am persuaded a particular account will be given to the public, of the memorable communion at Cambuslang last Lord's day, being the 15th of this current August, yet I cannot but here insert, that I observed much of the Lord's presence with ministers, and among the vast multitude of people there. There were many unconverted sinners awakened, and several had the love of God shed abroad in their hearts, by the Holy Ghost given to them, to such a measure that they were nigh overwhelmed therewith. Particularly while they were hearing, early upon Monday morning, a sermon preached by the Rev. Mr. Webster, minister at Edinburgh. One of them was a young woman, from the parish of Kilsyth. She was brought to me, at my first alighting at Cambuslang, after the sermon. She was so filled with a sense of the love of God to her soul, and with love to Jesus Christ, that she was all in tears and could not contain herself. She had been awakened at Kilsyth about the beginning of July, but had attained to no sensible relief untill hearing the aforesaid sermon. Before her awakening she was of a blameless life and every way hopeful. Her convictions were kindly and had a most desirable progress. I called for her yesterday, and she gave me a satisfying account of her closing with Christ in all his offices, and of her attainments, during the foresaid sermon, accompanied with such exercise of soul as we use warrantably to give from the Holy Scriptures as evidences of that which comes from God, in a saving manner, upon the souls of his people.

Having thus narrated what I have learned concerning the progress and extent of this good work since it began here, I shall, for the greater distinctness, divide the subject of this Narrative into the following Articles.

Chapter 2

Coping with Revival

THOUGH I am far from thinking the way I have used to be the very best, and from proposing it as a rule to any, seeing that by experience I have found out some mistakes in my management, which I afterwards rectified, and others possibly in perusing this may observe more; yet the success I had therein, and the hope that it may be useful at least to some of my younger brethren when they shall be called, as I pray they may be soon, to this pleasant service, induceth me to give the subject of this Chapter.

When the first extraordinary awakening of numbers took place in this congregation, though I knew the objections made against the outcries at Cambuslang and the bodily distresses many were under there, and was satisfied in my own mind that there was nothing in these objections; yet when I heard these outcries, and saw the bodily distresses some of the awakened were under, it proved at first very uneasy to me — it appeared unpleasant, yea even shocking; I therefore resolved, that as soon as any fell under remarkable distress they should be carried out of the congregation, into a separate place I had provided for them, and appointed some of the elders to carry, them off accordingly. I also prayed, that if it were the holy will of God, he would bring them to a sight of their sin and danger without these bodily distresses, which were so unpleasant to behold, so distressing to the people themselves, and offensive to several. The Lord in a little time discovered to me my error and imprudence in this. For after I had conversed for some time with the distressed, I found the distress of their minds to be so great as could not but naturally have such effects upon their bodies. I enquired at many of them, what they apprehended and felt in their minds before they fell a-trembling, cried out, or fainted. They told me, that they were under dreadful apprehensions of the terrible wrath of God, due to them for their sins, especially for their slighting of Jesus Christ by unbelief. This view made easy what before was shocking to me. I looked upon it as the effect of a due regard to the wrath of God, which sinners in a state of nature are under and liable to. I beheld them as enemies to the King of glory, falling under him, riding in his glory and majesty, and making his arrows sharply pierce their hearts. I found also that the congregation, instead of being disturbed with their outcries, were more disturbed by carrying them off; and the people's attention much lessened in hearing the word. Several left the place of hearing, and went where the distressed were, to gaze upon them. It was also a considerable inconvenience when there were no ministers here to direct and comfort the distressed, as they were left with those who could give them no assistance. The number of the awakened were much diminished, and came soon to be very few. I observed that some were awakened while they had the distressed in their sight, and heard exhortations given in the place where they were convened: from this I was persuaded, that the example of others under spiritual terrors and distress was one of the means the Lord was pleased to make use of to bring beholders to consider their own state and way, and to attend more carefully to what they heard from the word of God. Several of the awakened told me, that they were brought to a concern about their souls by such a reasoning as this within themselves: These people under so much distress are far from being so great sinners as I have been and am: how stupid and hard-hearted then am I who am altogether unconcerned. And if they be afraid of the wrath of God, I have far greater reason to be so. There appeared to me nothing more unreasonable in making use of the example of the distressed, to make other secure sinners afraid of sin and the wrath of God, than there is in the law punishing crimes publicly to make others afraid to commit them. I was also convinced that it was sinful in me to wish or desire that the infinitely wise and sovereign Lord should order his own work in an other way than what pleased himself. There were also some brethren who did not think the way I had taken, to remove the distressed, to be the best; and therefore, after some weeks' trial, I altered it: I am now of opinion, after all that I have seen and experienced relating to this work, that it is best to leave the distressed to their liberty, and in the congregation, if they incline, untill it be dismissed. No mean that Providence puts in our hands is to be omitted that hath a tendency to awaken secure sinners.

As to preaching the word of God upon work-days, I resolved at first only to have it upon the Wednesday, which we accordingly had. Some days we had three sermons, sometimes two, and at other times one, as the Lord provided instruments. Thus we continued for some weeks. I observed an uncommon earnest inclination in the people of all sorts to hear the word of God. I could not reasonably think that this would last long, and therefore I thought myself warranted, from the example of our Lord Jesus Christ, to have the word more frequently preached to them while they were so pressing and eager to attend to it. What determined me further to this was, that the sword of the Spirit was at no time now unsheathed but some were cut to the quick by it; as also, in other congregations, where weekly sermons were not set up, or but seldom kept, the people were awakened and this good work went on but slowly. I therefore embraced every opportunity of stranger ministers coming to the place to give sermon to the people; and that they who needed rather a bridle than a spur in hearing might not be hindered in their necessary worldly affairs, these sermons were ordinarily in the evening, when the day's work was near an end. These occasional sermons were never without some good fruit in awakening secure sinners, and also in comforting some who had been formerly awakened. I have never to this day heard of any parents or masters in this congregation who complained that their children or servants were drawn away from their duty by these means. Yea, this every day I made inquiry at some husbandmen, living in different parts of the parish, if now, when harvest has begun, they observed any part of the work and labour in the parish undone, or farther behind, through the frequent attendance upon public ordinances, or by the means of the many awakened and spiritually distressed in the congregation. They replied, that there was no such thing to be seen; as also, that they had heard the poorest say, that their work went better on than ordinary, and that they found not any lack. They observed also, that their hay harvest, which is a considerable labour in this parish, was got a third part of time sooner over than ordinary, and noticed the singular goodness of God therein.

As to the doctrines I preached in the congregation or elsewhere, there was as much as possible a mixture of the law and the gospel in the same sermon, and I observed such compositions most blessed of God. The formerly converted, and the awakened who had made progress, were, I perceived, most affected with the sweet truths of the gospel. I have seen the congregation in tears, and crying out, when the gospel of grace from mount Zion, without any express mixture of the terrors of the law, was preached. It is true indeed, that several of the awakened have had their spiritual distress increased thereby, as also some of the secure have been awakened: but then it was from their being convinced that they had as yet no interest in these glorious -blessings, and so were miserable, and that it would be the worst part of their eternal misery to be deprived of them! And thus it was as terrible to them to hear heaven preached of as hell, seeing they saw themselves shut out from it by their unbelief. I observed that the far greater part of every public audience were secure, unconcerned, and fearless, and therefore I preached the terrors of the law in the strongest terms I could, that is to say, in express scripture terms. I feared to daub or deal slightly with them, but told great and small, that they were the children of the Devil while they were in the state of unbelief, and that if they continued so to the end, in our Lord's plain terms, they would be damned. I resolved that I would cry aloud and not spare, and preach with that seriousness and fervour that became me as knowing that my hearers must either be prevailed with or be damned; and that they might discern I was in good earnest with them, and really meant as I spoke. And lest any should ascribe the effect of these sermons to the subject, I observed to my hearers frequently that they had often heard all these truths preached to them with as great keenness without any such visible effect. I can instance and show sermons containing the terrors of the law that I have preached many years ago without known success, but which I have again preached now, in weaker terms, with great success; so that all might see that it is not from man, but the Spirit of the Lord, that there is so great a difference as to efficacy.

I looked up and saw, what I never saw before, the fields already ripe unto harvest. I heard the Lord of the harvest commanding me to put in my sickle and reap; I considered that I had now put into my hand an opportunity that was not to last long, the harvest being the shortest time of labour in the whole year. And therefore I resolved to bestir myself and attend wholly to this very thing. I looked upon my pulpit-work, though great, as but a small part of my task. I knew that several of the awakened were ignorant, that all of them needed particular direction, instruction, and consolation, under their sharp convictions, and much wanted, under the conduct of the Holy Spirit, a spiritual guide to direct them to faith in Jesus Christ, to which they were shut up. I appointed therefore Monday, Tuesday, Thursday, and Friday, for the awakened and spiritually-distressed to come to me for the aforesaid purposes, which they did, assiduously and diligently, from morning to night; the same persons sometimes coming to me not only twice in the week, which was ordinary, but oftener; yea, even upon Saturdays, which I often grudged, but durst not send those away who had come from a distance without conversing with them. At this time I could not allow myself to be diverted from this attendance by any visitants coming to my house, ministers or others. I was also greatly assisted by some ministers and preachers who stayed with me for some time. Particularly at the beginning of this work, Mr. Young, preacher of the gospel, who had been much at Cambuslang, and had great experience and skill in dealing with the distressed, was greatly helpful to me. But of all others the Rev. Mr. Gillespie, minister of Carnock, was most remarkably *God's send* to me. He came to me upon the Monday before the Lord's Supper was given in the congregation, and stayed ten days. Both of us had as much work among the distressed as kept us continually employed from morning to night; and without him it would have been impossible for me to have managed the work of that week. Without such dealings with them, humanly speaking, many of them must have miscarried, or continued much longer under their spiritual distress. It is very true that God will devise means to bring home his banished, as I have seen: but where there are ministers, these are the outward means. If people in distress will not use them they themselves are to blame, and they cannot expect a desirable outgate. And if we will not apply ourselves diligently to the care of distressed souls willing to make use of us, the Lord will provide without us, that his own elect shall not miscarry; but woe will be to us — their blood, as well as those who shall miscarry, will be required at our hands.

I was not without temptations to slacken my hand. Both my own mind and others who wished me well said, Spare thyself. I was afraid my body would not stand through, and others told me I should take care of my health: But when I considered my natural temper, that it must be employed somehow, and that I spent nearly as much time in reading, I thought I could suffer no more by this application, and had not so much to fear from it as from any other constant sedentary employment. But most of all I was influenced from the consideration of the Lord's call to this service, that my time, health, and life were in his hand, that I had dedicated all to his service and glory, that he had promised needful strength — that he would preserve my health and life so long as he had use for them, and that it would be highly unreasonable for me to desire it longer, and I resolved not to spare myself. It became soon the pleasantest work ever I engaged in. I found the distressed profiting under the means of grace by the Lord's blessing, first coming to hate sin and mourn for it, out of a regard to God, and pressing after an interest in the Lord Jesus Christ. It diverted me to see young and old carrying their bibles with them, and either reading some passage that had been of use to them, or looking out and marking some passage I recommended to them. The world appeared changed to me, and as I noticed to them; for when I came to their doors, once or twice in the year, to catechise them, the least trifle hindered their attendance, but now they were glad to come twice or thrice a week, and greedy to receive instruction: and what cold soul would not have rejoiced at such a change, and welcomed them in the name of the Lord? Though I was wearied when I went to bed, yet, like the labouring man, my rest was sweet to me. The Lord gave me the sleep of his beloved, and I was fresh by the morning. And now, after labouring so much for nearly these four months, and preaching more than at any time for a whole half year, I mention it the praise of my Master's goodness, my body is like those of Daniel and the three children, fatter in flesh than when I began, and my bodily ails nowise encreased. The way of the Lord hath been my life and strength.

After sermon, those who were awakened that day were convened in my barn. Sometimes they were spoken to altogether, either by myself or some other minister, if any happened to be with us; as also, we prayed with them. This, as was observed already, had frequently, by the blessing of God, effect upon the by-standers; some being awakened by seeing the distressed and hearing the exhortations given in the barn. At other times, when I could not attend upon this, and there were no other ministers, some of the elders were sent to pray and sing psalms with them. They were then by the elders brought to me, into my closet, one by one, or if there were many, two or three at a time. If they were able to give an account of themselves, I enquired when they came first to be so deeply concerned about the state of their souls — what was the occasion of it — and what they had heard that made the first impression upon them. After which I gave them some general exhortations and directions suitable to their particular case, as the Lord was pleased to help.

The general exhortations and directions I gave them were to be very thankful to God, and bless him who had sent his Holy Spirit to convince them of sin because they believed not upon Christ, and to make them sensible of their lost state, that they might be delivered; to entertain a constant fear lest their convictions and uneasy sense of their sin and danger should go off without conversion and coming to Christ by faith, seeing this had befallen many who had been under greater and longer distress than many of them yet were; and that if this happened to them their case would be worse and more dangerous than it was before: And therefore they should take good heed that they resist not the convictions of the Spirit, but listen to them and admit them to take possession of their soul; that they need not be overwhelmed, for how great soever their sins were, if they would repent and believe upon the Lord Jesus Christ, God promised to have mercy upon them and save them; and that they must not be too impatient for comfort, nor too hasty to catch it, but that they must stay God's time, and wait upon him patiently, in a diligent use of means, for a good issue. I prayed with them, and so dismissed them, without being more particular with them for the first time. Several of them, through the greatness of their anguish, were not able even to attend to such short and general directions. I recommended it to strangers to apply frequently to their own ministers for instruction and direction under their spiritual distress, trusting that there would be no minister, wherever they were awakened, who would not make them welcome, instruct, and direct them to Jesus Christ. I endeavoured yet to persuade myself that the jealousy some of the distressed entertain of a bad reception is groundless. It were to be wished that ministers who hear of any such in their congregation would enquire after them, desire them to come to them from time to time, and thereby convince them that their jealousies are groundless, that they compassionate their case and are ready to assist them under the pangs of the new birth, that they may not miscarry. Nothing so tender as an afflicted conscience; those who have it must be tenderly dealt and borne with. Let us all who are called to the holy ministry often think upon Ezek. xxxiv, 4.

As to the method of my after-dealing with the awakened, as they came to me from time to time, this cannot be well narrated without giving an account of the progress of the work of conviction upon them, and therefore I shall refer it to that Article.

I have kept a book in which, from day to day, I wrote down what was most material in the exercises of the distressed. This may appear an insupportable labour at first view, especially where the number of the distressed were so many. Yet I found it to be very easy: it saved much time to me. An index I kept brought me soon to the part of the book where the person's case was recorded. I had then a full view of their case as it was when they were first with me. I saw what progress their convictions had made, and knew where I was to begin with them, without examining their case every time from the beginning anew, as otherwise I would have been obliged to do: which would have taken three or four times more time than I needed to spend with them. It after all gave a full view of their whole case when it came to an issue; and made me more able to judge it.

I have laboured to be very cautious in pronouncing persons to be brought out of a state of nature into a state of grace. I have in many cases declared to persons, that the grounds of ease and rest they took up with were not solid nor good, which frequently had a good effect; and as to others, that if their exercises were such as they declared them to be, they were really the scripture qualifications and experiences of the converted. But of this more in another Chapter.

It made all this labour more pleasant to me, that the Lord, even from the first week, brought some every week to satisfying relief by faith in the Lord Jesus. The first appearance of this filled me with tears of joy. It was in a girl about twenty, the first week after the 16th of May.

An abstract of her case is as follows: She formerly lived for some years in this parish, but at this time in the neighbourhood. She was first brought under some concern at Cambuslang, by hearing Luke, xi, 21, preached upon. She was afraid the Lord had passed her by when she saw others under spiritual distress. She wondered what convictions were when she heard them spoken of, and prayed for them. She was further awakened to see her sin and danger at Kilsyth, upon the 16th of May. She returned to me the same week. I was greatly pleased with the progress of her convictions, with her knowledge, and the longing desires she expressed after Jesus Christ. I said to her, sitting by me, essay to accept of the Lord Jesus Christ, bestir yourself, rise up at his call, and invite him to enter into your soul; without intending or meaning what she did. She arose with great composure, stood and prayed in a scripture style, and with such connection as no person of a public character needed to have been ashamed of before the most critical. I could discern as much of the spirit of grace and adoption in it as any prayer I ever heard. I could not recover it afterwards; but resolved that I would desire her to pray the next time she returned: For I looked upon her as having received the spirit of faith, though she continued disconsolate. Next week she returned: and I caused her to pray after I had conversed and prayed with her. She did it in a scripture style, with connection, and great earnestness; acknowledging sin, original and actual; her utter want of righteousness, and the wonderfulness of God's patience towards her: she prayed for mercy to be drawn to Jesus Christ, and that she might be clothed with his white raiment; that he would speak a word in season to her weary, heavy-laden, and burdened soul; and that he would give her to come to him, who saith, "Come to me, all ye that are weary and heavy-laden, and I will give you rest;" that Satan might have no interest in her; and that the Lord would do for her above all she could ask, think, or crave; giving glory to him who liveth for ever. Sometimes in her address she said, Sweet Jesus. She first came to sensible relief, the next week, in hearing a sermon I preached from John, xvi, 10. In her return home, by herself, these words were strongly impressed upon her, "My heart is fixed, O God, my heart is fixed; I will sing and give praise." She fell down upon her knees, her heart being filled with joy in the Lord and her mouth with his praise. She said that, May 16th, when she was under her greatest distress, the last verses of the fortieth of Isaiah came to her remembrance, "They that wait upon the Lord shall renew their strength; they shall mount up with

68

wings as eagles, they shall run and not be weary, they shall walk and not faint." This gave her some support and encouragement to wait upon the Lord.

There were some disorders I could not foresee; but as soon as they appeared, I was careful to destroy them in the bud, and prevent them in time to come. Many, when they saw the great fears and anguish of those awakened upon the 16th of May, concluded that they were sinners above all others, and that they had been guilty of some sins more than ordinary, which came now to give them so much uneasiness. They entertained a notion, that if they would confess these extraordinary sins, it would give ease to their minds, and glorify God. This was followed with very bad consequences. One was, that some, through these mistakes, attacked some of the awakened under their greatest agonies and while they knew not what to do, and exhorted them to confess all their sins, and tell them what they had done that so vexed them, which might turn to their ease. One poor woman, who was awakened upon the 16th of May, but went home without speaking with me, came to be in such agonies that her neighbours were obliged to watch with her all night, and she, being dealt with as above, acknowledged that she had been guilty of adultery with a man she also named. She had been of an evil character for cursing, scolding, and living ill with her husband, but nobody had suspected her being unchaste. She was brought to me early next morning. When I heard the story it gave me great uneasiness, but there was no preventing the spreading of it — it was reported through the neighbourhood by the morning light. I heard also of attempts of the same kind made upon some others, but without reproachful consequences. To prevent this for the time to come, I publicly instructed the whole congregation that they were not bound to confess their secret sins to any but unto God, unless in case of his bringing them to light in his providence; or in the case of wrong and injury done their neighbours, where reparation or satisfaction should be made, and brotherly forgiveness sought; or in case of great vexation of mind, and want of advice for relief about some particular sin, that they should do it to some minister, or prudent Christian friend, who would keep it as an inviolable secret to the day of judgment: forbidding, at the same time, all to enquire into the secret sins of their neighbours: showing unto them the evil of it; and most of all, their blazing abroad the secret faults of their neighbour, when it could tend to no end but the reproach of their neighbour and the scandal and offence of others. This warning, by the Lord's blessing, prevented any disorder of this sort for the time to come. There was another evil consequence of this mistake, that many — though all the first awakened were of blameless lives except the foresaid woman — imagining that they were troubled for some uncommon sin, were thereby hardened against convictions, whilst they knew not themselves to be guilty of any sin more than ordinary. They never reflected upon the evil of the least sin, and upon the dreadful evil of rejecting Jesus Christ by unbelief, worse than the greatest sin against the law. These things were observed to them in preaching and private conferences; but I am persuaded this had no great influence untill the Lord was pleased to awaken several of the young ones, of whom they could have no jealousy, that they have been sinners above all others. This served effectually to remove the foresaid stumbling-block; and several came to reason the other way, that if such young ones, comparatively innocent, were brought under such deep concern about their sin and misery, how much reason had they to be affected, let them be ever so free from gross sins.

There were some other disorders that were like to arise in this and neighbouring congregations that were timeously noticed, rectified, or prevented; and the people in this congregation came willingly under very strict and exact rules for the management of this affair.

What made me in every thing to use the more caution was, that I was persuaded the further progress this blessed work should make, the greater opposition would be made to it; and the more Christ should triumph, the more Satan would rage, which I now see has come to pass. For Satan seemed to be astonished with the first appearance at Cambuslang, so as not to know well by what methods to oppose it, but now recovers and rallies all his forces to make head. The Seceders made the most opposition at the first, and that even in a fainter and wavering way. But now Nullifidians of all sorts are making head, such as Arians, who deny the supreme Deity of our Lord and Saviour, and the satisfaction he hath given to the justice of God for elect sinners; Arminians, who have never been friendly to the scripture doctrine of justification by faith alone without the works of the law, and of the sinner's regeneration and conversion by the supernatural power of the Holy Ghost. And, last of all, those who cry up morality without the faith and hope of the gospel and that love to God that is engendered by it; and so, out of fondness for Pagan ethics and philosophic institutions, defy our holy religion. There are strong presumptions that the anonymous pamphlets now flying so thick are from that sort. And no wonder; for the progress of this work threatens shame and destruction to all their darling principles and practices.

Chapter 3

The Effect of the Revival

THE fruits of this remarkable out-pouring of the Holy Spirit are either general, extending to the body of the people, or more particular, the awakening of many to an uneasy sight of their sin and danger, the conversion of some of those who were visibly awakened, the hopeful condition of some others of the awakened, and the reviving and attainments of former good Christians.

The first of these is the subject of the Chapter. Among the instances of the good fruits of this work upon the generality of the people are the visible reformation from many open sins in their lives: particularly cursing and swearing and minced oaths, which formerly were frequent, but are now laid aside. Drinking to excess is either forborne or much discountenanced. In public occasional meetings, edifying discourse hath taken the place of frothy, foolish, censorious, or otherwise evil speaking. Instead of worldly and common discourse upon the Lord's day, there is that which is spiritual and good to the use of edifying. There is little of sitting idle at their doors, and profanely strolling in the streets on that day, which was too common formerly in the town of Kilsyth. There is a general desire after public ordinances; and whereas before this I never could prevail with the best to attend the preaching of the word upon work days, and therefore could have no stated weekly day for this, they now desire it, and the generality of the people frequent it as regularly as upon the Lord's day. The worship of God is set up and daily kept up in many families which were known entirely to neglect it aforetime. There are many societies formed for prayer in the parish, both of old and young, and these not only of persons who have been awakened at this time, but of others. Former feuds and animosities are in a great measure laid aside and forgotten, and this hath been the most peaceable summer amongst our neighbours that was ever known in these bounds. I have heard little or nothing of that pilfering and stealing that was become so frequent and uneasy before this work began. Yea, there have been several instances of restitution, and some of these showing consciences more than ordinarily tender. The change of the face of our public meetings for worship is visible; there were never such attention and seriousness to be seen in them as now. The change of the lives of the generality to the better is observed by every one who knew the place. One observing person in the congregation said lately to me, that he was sure, if there was nothing more, there was more morality among them. It is strange that some who make so much noise about morality should be such enemies to a work which hath produced so much of it in the lives of a whole country-side.

Chapter 4

Silent and Unobserved

THE first general distinction of the awakened for some months past in this congregation is into those who have been brought into a deep concern about the state of their souls without being known or observed by others, untill they attained such relief as gives ground to judge it solid and scriptural, and those whose concern and awakening was notorious, and observed by all who saw them, from its sensible effects upon them.

The first sort belong to this Chapter. Some have declared, their greatest dissatisfaction with this work was that the awakened did not conceal, at least from the public, their spiritual distress, and that so much noise was made about it; and they would have been pleased with instances of a work of conviction and conversion carried on in a calm, silent, and quiet manner. In all this they have the satisfaction they demand, and at the same time an evidence of more than an ordinary out-pouring of the Holy Spirit, wherewith they should also be satisfied, seeing that the instances are more numerous these six months past than they have been for as many years before, as far as I can judge; and these instances of conversion more unquestionable.

Blessed be the God of peace and of all grace, there are not a few in this congregation, known to me at this time, who have within these six months been awakened to a serious concern about their souls' salvation, brought under a deep work of humiliation, and appear, as far as I am able to judge, to be converted; and yet, as to some of them, their spiritual distress and exercises, while they were under them, were not known to me or to any else, and as to others, only to some very intimate and near friend. I had occasion to converse with some of them before the giving of the Lord's Supper in the congregation in the month of July last. Others I have called for and enquired into the state of their souls and their experiences. And some have given me an account of themselves in writing, whom I have also enquired after and conversed closely with. And I hope there are a considerably greater number upon whom the Lord is carrying on a good work of grace in this still and unobserved manner. The general concern there is in hearing the word of God, and diligence in the use of means, joined with outward reformation, give great ground to hope this.

Those of this sort with whom I have conversed have had convictions, fears, distresses, and exercises of the same kind with those whose distresses have been manifested openly, and their experiences, as to an escape by grace, have been much alike.

I shall insert the account some of these gave me of themselves in this Chapter, and leave it to the reader to judge for himself.

The first instance is contained in the second printed Journal from Kilsyth, which is as follows:

C. D. came first under convictions, which made him uneasy, upon the first Sabbath of March last. By hearing the work of regeneration preached, as it is the writing of God's law upon the sinner's heart, from Heb. viii, 10, he was made to see that it was not as yet written upon his heart, and the absolute necessity of having it. At night his landlady and he discoursed of God's raising the dead at the general judgment. The consideration of these, and of the dreadful state which the wicked shall be in, made further deep impressions upon him. He says, that he found every sermon he heard made these impressions deeper; and that he was much displeased with himself that his concern and anxiety about his spiritual and eternal state was not greater. Upon the last Sabbath of April his convictions, and thereby his distress, came to a great height, from his hearing of a woman who was that day awakened, and brought to my house in great distress.

He told me, that he could apply to himself the most part of a sermon he heard from me upon the 19th of May last, concerning the Spirit's convincing the world of sin; such as, that he usually begins with one sin, and carrieth it on to a conviction of particular sins: which, he says, he could name particularly before the Lord: and that further, he was convinced of bosom sins, and of the evil nature of sin; and that he was not so much affrighted with the terror of hell as he was afflicted for offending a holy God. And that further, he got such a sight of the filthiness of sin, as to loathe himself because of it. That he was also convinced of the evil of unbelief, of the first motions of sin, and the sinfulness of them, though not consented to; of self-conceit, a sense of the evil of which stuck as long with him as any thing else, as he terms it. He was also convinced of his inability to help himself, and of his own want of righteousness, and that he could never work out righteousness for himself. He says further, that he was brought to see the sufficiency of Christ and his righteousness, and that he was always ready (which are his own words) if he could but trust in him.

Seeing he had told me, that he had never informed any person of his inward spiritual distress untill he got an outgate, I asked him, what it was that kept up his spirit under fear and trouble of mind continuing so long. He answered, that when his heart was like to burst in prayer, that word in the fourtieth Psalm and first verse came constantly into his mind — "I waited patiently for the Lord, and he inclined unto me, and heard my cry;" and that this encouraged him to wait for the Lord with patience and hope.

His first relief came after this manner: In the society for prayer, to which he had joined himself, he enquired, What is the most proper exercise for a person under convictions? It was answered him by a judicious Christian, that it was to behold the Lamb of God who taketh away the sin of the world, which he essayed to do.

Upon the Sabbath after that, I gave the marks of those who have Christ formed in them; such as having the Spirit of Christ, 1 John, iii, 24; Saving faith, Eph. iii, 17; Devoting and dedicating ourselves to the Lord, Rom. vi, 13; Impressions answerable to the mediatory actions of Jesus Christ, Rom. vi, 4–6; Habitual endeavour to imitate him, 1 John, ii, 6; Fervent longings after a perfect likeness to him, Phil. iii, 8–13; And lastly, A high value for the word and institutions of Jesus Christ. He says, that by the help of the Spirit he could apply them all to himself. And that during the public prayer after sermon, he was in a frame surprising to himself: that his whole heart and affections went out in closing with Jesus Christ; and that he was filled with rejoicing and wonder at his love.

During that night and two days after, he was much dejected and cast down, for fear that things were not right with him, and lest it was not a real work of grace upon him.

He got out of this plunge, by the third verse of the sixth chapter of Hosea, brought to his remembrance while he was retired: "Then shall we know, if we follow on to know the Lord: his going forth is prepared as the morning; and he shall come unto us as the rain; as the latter and former rain upon the earth." It was some days after that ere he could find these words out. He was then filled with joy in the Lord, and wonder at his love, and thought he could do and suffer any thing for Jesus Christ, who had done and suffered so much for him. He came to be satisfied about the truth of the work of grace upon him, and to be free from doubts about his interest; which, he says, continues in some good measure with him, and that though he is sometimes dull, as he calls it; yet he is not a day to an end without some reviving.

The above relation was made me by the foresaid person upon the 27th of May last in my closet, his conversation appears to all who know him to be sober, pious, and suitable to the narrative given.

The person concerned in this Journal continues, by grace, this 16th of September, to walk tenderly, and in every instance of life as becometh a good Christian.

I have not taken down the relation others of this sort have given me of their case. There is one who comes near this class, seeing he never applied to any minister, and opened his distress to few, if to any, while he was under it. He lives upon the borders of this parish, and attends ordinarily public ordinances, here because of his great distance from his own parish church. He put a paper into my hand, upon Sabbath the 8th of August, which he desired me to peruse at leisure. I found it to contain an account of God's dealing with his soul. It was written and subscribed by him, at his dwelling-house, August 5th. I shall subjoin an abstract of it, giving his own words for the most part.

He says, he was much troubled untill he made known to me what the Lord hath bestowed of his infinite mercy upon him since the Lord's Supper was given in this congregation. That first of all, while he was hearing the action sermon preached from Zech. ix, 11, he was made to see himself bound in that pit "wherein there is no water." And thought in his mind as if one had spoken to him these words, "Believe or thou shalt be damned;" upon which he fell into great trouble of mind. When Mr. Thomas Gillespie exhorted the last table, and told the worthy communicants, that God and Christ were theirs, heaven and earth were theirs, Bible and ministers were theirs, he thought he had no right to anything that was good. And being gone home, he wept all night. He writes further in these words. "Coming to the church on Monday, when Mr. Mackie closed the work he expressed these words, 'O bless God, unworthy communicants, that he is still waiting to be gracious to you, although you have trampled his Son's blood under your feet.' That word gave me some comfort. And when he was done, ye gave some directions, saying, Did we not envy them that were going home with Christ in their bosom, and we have the Devil in ours? And earnestly entreated us to part with the Devil, and take Christ. At which words, I thought I saw the Devil in my own bosom. I came to your barn, and these words came into my heart, 'Thou art damned already;' and I came home; for I thought it folly to speak to any minister, for my case was past hope. And I prayed that the Lord would not cast me into hell, till I gave him thanks for all his mercies I had received since I came into this world. And since I must be damned, I prayed that the Lord would save all others, and I would be content to go to hell myself alone. In this sad condition, and much worse than I can tell, I continued for some time. And lying on my bed one night bewailing my condition:" Afterwards he speaks of impressions of pardon, his concern about confession of sin, and the continuance of these impressions of pardon, till he fell asleep, and adds, "When I awaked all my comfort was gone, and I would have given a thousand worlds for one smile again: but there is no tongue can tell such grief and love my heart did burn with. Methought my heart would break, when I thought on the great love and good-will of Heaven to mankind sinners; considering my own unworthiness, that ere ever I had thought of mercy he showed me such kindness. O if I had ten thousand hearts I would do nought else but show forth his praise! Likewise, I heard a minister preach at your church on these words, 'Grieve not the Holy Spirit of God, whereby ye are sealed unto the day of redemption.' And another scripture cited, 'Quench not the Spirit.' These two scriptures did me much good. So when any good thought comes into my mind, I look into the scripture, and if I find it there; I endeavour to keep it; and if I do not, I let it go, as not consistent with the word of God. Blessed be God, I take more delight in striving to please him than ever I did to please my own evil conceit and fulfilling my worldly lust. I had a great mind to go to the Lord's table at the sacrament in our own church: but I thought, that surely my sins were not yet repented of; for I saw many persons sore and long troubled that I was sure were not so great sinners as I, and I had not suffered the one half that they had. That word was put in my heart, 'Wilt thou eat my flesh, and drink my blood, and hast no part in me?' At which words I almost despaired of mercy for the space of two days. And while I lamented my condition in prayer to God, these words were engraven in my heart, 'He that doubteth shall be damned; for thy sins are forgiven thee; why dost thou this?' These words made me as strong in love to my Redeemer as ever. So I went to the Lord's table; and received great and unspeakable comfort, and coming home I could speak to no man; my heart was so ravished with joy; for I found that the Lord was reconciled to my soul. As I was praying in the fields at night, there came such a fear on me that I could not speak, but trembled. Then I thought it was said to me, 'Fear not, I am betrothed unto thee:' so all that slavish fear left me, and I praised God with joy. Sometimes if I were praying, I can get nothing said, but, O love, O love, redeeming love! And these impressions of God's love will come upon me so that I must retire from all company for a little. And you being the instrument in God's hand of first awakening me, I could not rest till I revealed it to you, desiring always your prayers, that God would enable me to perform the duty called for at my hand. I have written this, because you have no time to discourse with me. Blessed be God, that ever I heard you preach one sermon."

Upon the 23rd of August last, he put another paper into my hand of that day's date, a part of which is as follows.

"Sir, Since the 8th to the 15th day of this month, I have been under great distress of mind. For sometimes I thought, that I was sure of the Lord's favour, and at other times put in great doubt, for that the Lord was so just that he would assuredly render unto every man according as his works should be; but that blessed scripture, as a smile from the Lord's own mouth, was impressed on my heart, "Come and let us reason together; though your sins be as crimson, I will make them white as snow." "Believe on the Son of God, and it is impossible for thee to be damned." But alas! my heart put me in great doubt, by reason that all these lively and heart-admiring thoughts of my Redeemer vanished away, and my heart grew as hard as a stone, and I could see no loveliness in him for which he was to be desired. So in this melancholy condition I went to the sacrament at Cambuslang, and being at the table, the Rev. Mr. Whitefield expressed these words, 'O dear Redeemer, seal these lambs of thine to the day of redemption.' At which words my breath was near stopping, and the blood gushed at my nose. He said, Be not afraid, for God shall put up thy tears in this bottle. These words were put into my heart, 'A new heart will I give you, and a right spirit will I put within you' &c. I sat afterwards at the table overjoyed with the love of my dear Redeemer. This is my petition unto you, that you would give me some directions: for sometimes my heart is as cold as ever it was in all my life, and will struggle as with one that is stronger than I, and would almost give over to the world again if his mercy did not prevent me. And I am greatly afraid that the Lord will let me fall into the hand of my greatest enemies, and then my last state shall be worse than the first. I entreat you, as a well-wisher to my soul, to give me some directions against this doubting spirit that is in me; for sometimes the love I bear in my heart to my Redeemer, and the love that I conceive that he hath to me and to all who love him with unfeigned hearts, is so great that I am obliged to pray, to hold his hand, for I am overfilled with his love. And at other times I am lukewarm and indifferent: though I would pray till I could speak no more, all is in vain till the Lord be pleased to blow again upon my soul."

I conversed with him this day, and found that he had a pretty distinct knowledge of the sinner's way of relief by faith in the Lord Jesus. He professed that he had accepted a whole Christ. And he looked for acceptance with God, not on the account of his repentance or duties, but only of Christ's righteousness. And that he was sorry for his past sins, and resolved against sin, in Christ's strength, from the time to come.

I enquired at him the meaning of some expressions of his paper. Particularly his praying to be allowed to confess his sins, &c. He said that he did not think himself enough grieved for sins, nor sufficiently humbled to believe upon Christ. Which hath been the temptation and mistake of many distressed souls, they have imagined such a measure of humiliation, without which they conceived they had no warrant to believe upon the Lord Jesus Christ, not considering that humiliation is no warrant or ground to believe, but needful in the hand of the Spirit to make sinners willing to part with all sin, and believe upon the Lord Jesus.

He and another with him, who had also sent me in writing a relation of the exercises of his soul, complained bitterly of the hardness of their hearts at that time. I found that they understood by the hardness of their hearts, the want sometimes of a great motion of their affections, and lively feelings of sin, misery, mercy, &c., and of fears as sometimes they had them. I told them that persons might have their affections and concerns about spiritual things greatly moved, and yet be really hard-hearted in the scripture sense; and others might be without fears and a great stir upon their affections, and yet have gracious, soft, and tender hearts: And that, if they were willing to have Christ and grace, and to forsake all their known sins, and to comply with the whole will of God made known to them, and were affected suitably with spiritual things, they had not the hard heart which is so much spoken against and condemned in scripture, and which usually means an untractable, disobedient, and an obstinate will to the will of God. And with this they were comforted.

This is a frequent complaint with many others when they cannot feel their affections and passions moved in the same degree they felt when they first closed with Christ, though their wills continue as persuadable, tractable, and obedient as when their affections were most lively.

Besides those I cam formerly to the knowledge of, which belong to this Article, several others of the same sort have been discovered to me in the month of September last, while I conversed with them, in order to their admission to the Lord's table. I had a remarkable instance of one on Saturday last, being the ninth of this current October. He came to speak with me upon a particular affair; I took occasion from it to enquire into the state of his soul, having never heard of his being under any concern about it. To my great surprise, he gave me an account of the beginning and progress of such a work upon him as appeared to me exceedingly hopeful. Having time and leisure I wrote it down. And seeing some of my friends desire I would give more instances in this Article, I shall add this to those already given.

W. X., formerly careless, and far from being circumspect and blameless in his walk, saith, that in the month of March, upon a certain Sabbath, when I was lecturing upon the history of Christ's life, he was tempted to think there was no such thing as I read and explained, and that there was no God: this filled him with great trouble. When he came home the temptation ceased, and he became easy.

Next Lord's day some concern about the state of his soul began with him. When he went about family worship after sermon, he thought the Bible was dearer to him than ever before; and he began to see somewhat of his vileness by sin, which continued with an increased upon him, from time to time, while I preached several sermons from Gal. iv, 19. His constant desire, wherever he went or whatever he did, was to have Christ formed in him.

When I was at Cambuslang, May 13th, he was there, and was, to his own feeling, brought under fear of God's wrath because of sin. He saith, when he heard the cries of the spiritually-distressed, he would have given a world to have been from amongst them: but thought with himself, though he might get from amongst them, yet he could not flee the judgment of God. He thought there was not so vile a sinner as he in the congregation. He saith, though he did not cry, or have any appearance of bodily trouble, yet he was in a flood of tears, and his heart was as if it would have bursted through his side. It was his great grief that he had sitten under the gospel-offer all his days, and never had given heed to it, but slighted and rejected it; of all which he was now clearly convinced.

Upon the 16th of May, he was made to see himself to be the vilest sinner present in the congregation, and that hell was ready to receive him as his due. He went home in great inward distress, retired to a chamber by himself, cried out in the anguish of his soul, and betook himself to prayer, Psalm lxii, 5, as in the metre, came to his mind.

> "My soul, wait thou with patience
> Upon thy God alone.
> On him dependeth all my hope
> And expectation."

This remained with him a long time. His convictions continued and increased, so that he was made to see many particular sins he was guilty of, which he never thought upon before; but especially slighting Christ by unbelief. He saith, that from the beginning of his concern, he was convinced of the corruption of his nature, and that he was born a natural enemy to God: and that as to sorrow for sin, though he was convinced that he deserved God's wrath, yet the principal reason of his sorrow was, that he had offended God and slighted Christ: and that he cannot speak of this, to this day, without heart-breaking.

In the end of May, or beginning of June, while he was at his work with others, he was seized with a great fear anent his state, and his being under the wrath of God because of sin. He retired to a private place, and attempted to pray. He could get nothing said but "O for Christ formed in me!" He returned to his work, and while he was employed in it, he was convinced that hitherto he had built his hope upon his own righteousness, and sought to be justified by his own works; and that he had all along thought it was well with him upon this ground. He retired again, got more liberty in prayer, and bewailed his former confidence in his own works and duties. After this he was let into a sight of his heart sins: he imagined he might get mercy notwithstanding of his outward sins; but wondered if any got mercy who had committed such heart sin as he.

When the Rev. Mr. Gillespie, minister of Carnock, preached here, about the beginning of July, from Heb. vii, 25, he was made to see the sufficiency of Christ's righteousness, and thought if he had a thousand souls he would venture them all upon it. These words uttered, "Christ hath shed his blood for thee," made deep impression upon him, and he endeavoured to throw himself upon it. He found some degree of love to Christ, and joy in him. Next morning he was dejected, from a view of his former profane life, and thought his former attainment was but a flash, because he could find no evidence in himself. His dejected frame continued with him to the Lord's day following, when the holy supper was given in the congregation.

Upon the morning of the said day, he rose early, and went to the fields. After prayer and much consideration there, he resolved not to go to the Lord's table, seeing he had so often formerly trampled upon Christ's blood by unworthy communicating. In his way homeward, he was afraid to stay away from the Lord's table, because it would be disobedience to Christ's dying command, and he was afraid to come, lest he should eat and drink unworthily. The former scripture, "O my soul, wait thou upon thy God with patience," came into his mind, as also, "I will go on in strength of God the Lord." He returned again to prayer; but after all he came to the church quite unresolved. During the action sermon, preached from Zech. ix, 11, he was made to see himself unworthy, vile, and deserving of damnation; he thought he would cast himself upon Christ, resolving in his strength against sin, and if he perished, he resolved to perish lying at the feet of his mercy. He saith, that towards the end of the sermon, I said that Christ in the gospel-offer was the rope let down to draw them out of that pit wherein there is no water, and I cried to sinners to catch hold of this rope: his heart was then enabled to accept and take hold of Christ, to his apprehension, in the sincerest manner: he was ravished with love to the Lord Jesus Christ, and found his soul so altered that he was persuaded the Lord Jesus was come into his heart. He went to the Lord's table, and saith that he found his heart contrary to whatever it was before, and that this contrariety continues with him. I enquired at him, wherein he observed this contrariety. He answered, he found a heart-hatred at all sin, and was more afraid of sin than of hell. And whereas before he had no delight in hearing, reading, or in prayer, but these were a burden to him: now they are his delight. Whereas formerly he had no concern about love to Christ: now he hath it for his continual grief, that he cannot get a heart to love the blessed Jesus enough. Formerly any formal duties he did he thought them good and right enough: now he sees the continual need of the blood of Christ to wash away the guilt of his best duties, and to be the ground of his acceptance in the sight of God. Formerly he had no regard to the laws of Jesus Christ: now he sees them all to be so just and right, that he wonders at his own wickedness in breaking such just laws. Formerly he saw no need of the Holy Spirit to sanctify and enable him to repent, believe, and do holy duties, and never had the least thought about this: he now cries for the teachings of the Holy Spirit, and his grace to enable him.

During a sermon preached by the Rev. Mr. Webster, minister of Edinburgh, from Eph. i, 7, upon the Wednesday thereafter at Kilsyth, he was further filled with peace and joy in believing. He continues for the most part in this comfortable situation. Sometimes he is greatly troubled with inclinations to self-righteousness, and with vain thoughts in the time of hearing, which are his grief and burden. He saith, it is his great concern that this blessed work make progress through the whole land, out of love to the glory of God and the salvation of souls, and that the kingdom of Jesus may be advanced.

There can be no objection taken from public outcries or bodily distresses, or having recourse to despised ministers for direction under spiritual distress, made against those in this Article, of whom I have given only a few instances, though able to give many more if it shall be found needful. I shall therefore proceed to narrate the case of those from whose circumstances the principal objects against this blessed work have been taken, and

leave all to the judgment of the Christian and unpre-
judiced reader.

Chapter 5

Some Cried Out

THEY are greatly mistaken who imagine that all those who have been observably awakened in this or in other congregations have come under faintings, temblings, or other bodily distress. These have been by far the fewest number. As far as I and others can judge, they have not been one to six. Others have indeed cried out when their spiritual distress came to a height, and some cried not out at all, with whom, notwithstanding their inward distress was so great that they were obliged to apply to me and the ministers to whose charge they belonged, for advice and direction.

This article gives instances of these two sorts, as they are distinguished from the first sort mentioned.

There was a great variety in the expressions uttered by those who cried out in public. Their different outcries were such as these: I am undone. What shall I do? "What shall I do to be saved?" "Lord, have mercy upon me." Oh, alas, O this unbelieving heart of mine. Some cried out bitterly, without uttering any words. Others restrained crying out while they were in public, who did it bitterly after they retired to their homes, and sometimes in their way homeward, and thereby gave no disturbance to the public preaching of the word, as those disorderly hearers (in the judgment of the adversaries to this blessed work) gave to Peter's sermon, according to the history of the second chapter of the Acts. Though indeed, I must acknowledge, I would be glad to be disturbed every sermon I preach by the outcries of all the Christless persons hearing me, if so were the will of God, to give them such a sight of their sin and danger as must break out into immediate and undelayed inquiries after the way of escape. Let those that never saw their own miserable condition in the light of a clear and full conviction, wonder to see or hear of others so deeply distressed in spirit as to make such outcries; I do not; because I am sure spiritual troubles do not exceed the cause and ground of them, let them be as great and deep as they will. And if others have had the effect of conversion, by the power of God's Spirit, in a gentler way; or, have had the discovery of the remedy as soon as the misery, which must needs prevent a great part of this trouble; let them not misjudge others, and set themselves up as standards; seeing that they are strangers to the doctrine of conversion, and the experiences of the Lord's people, who know not that God's ways of working in this are various, and different as to circumstances, though producing the same blessed effect.

The instances I give of those belonging to this Article are, first of all, the fourth and the ninth Journals from Kilsyth, in the Weekly History, printed at Glasgow. Both of these persons continue to the 19th of October to walk in the fear of the Lord, and comforts of the Holy Ghost. The woman hath had several more than ordinary sheddings abroad of the love of God in her heart, by the Holy Ghost given unto her.

Fourth Journal from Kilsyth.

G. H., of a blameless life, and an ordinary communicant for some years past, was awakened on May 16th; her spiritual distress was considerably great. The keeping a journal of the progress of the work of God upon her was omitted when she came to me from time to time.

June 8th, She was with me, and told me, it was better with her than when she was with me on the 4th current. She said she was somewhat comforted by the instructions the Lord directed me to give her that day; and began to be cheerful that night. Upon the Saturday, she was filled with doubts and fears, lest she was building upon a false foundation, and was so uneasy at night that she could not sleep. Upon the Lord's day, her spiritual distress increased to a great height. In her way home, she was greatly afraid lest death should seize her before she got to Christ. She sat down by the way, and composed herself to spiritual meditation, when the following scripture came into her mind with great power, "Be still, and know that I am God;" the effect of which was, that it composed her to wait with patience untill the Lord's time should come to relieve her, and that she was free from distressing doubts and fears that disturbed her, and was composed in prayer.

Upon the Monday, while she was employed in her worldly affairs, she thought that she could have been content to be constantly employed in praising God. All that while that word as strongly enforced upon her, "Be still and know that I am God." — In the evening, while she was late at her wheel in her master's house, the following scriptures were impressed upon her: "Fear not, for I am with thee; be not dismayed, for I am thy God: When thou passest through the waters, I will be with thee; and through the rivers, they shall not overflow thee: when thou walkest through the fire thou shalt not be burnt; neither shall the flame kindle upon thee. I will deliver thee in six troubles; yea, in seven there shall no evil touch thee." She found her heart begin to rise so with wonder at the mercy of God that she was ready to cry out in his loud praises. She rose and ran to her own chamber, situate upon one end of her master's house, and broke out in the praise of God. She was so much filled with love to Christ, and views of the greatness of his love to her, that she was overwhelmed with them. It was said to her, "Daughter, be of good cheer, for thy sins are forgiven thee," which filled her so with joy that she could not contain it: she cried out, "Unto him that loved us, and washed us from our sins in his blood, and hath made us kings and priests unto God and his Father; to him be glory and dominion for ever and ever. Amen." She says, she thought she could not cry loud enough to express his praises, thinking that all that was within her was but too little to do it, and that she was so over-whelmed that her heart was like to come out; yet felt no pain but much sweetness. When her master came to her, she cried out, "Come, all ye that fear the Lord, and I will tell you what he hath done for my soul;" and said, "that if all they whoever were or shall be were present, she would think it too little to tell it to them; and if they who opposed this work of the Spirit of God were present, she would tell it to his praise if they should kill her (her master told me he heard these expressions): she said, that she was composed in a while afterwards; but could not be satisfied, is not satisfied, nor ever will be satisfied with uttering his praises.

She proceeded further, and said to me, that she would lay her mouth in the dust, and be deeply humbled before the Lord so long as she lives, and that she thinks she could lie down with Mary at Christ's feet, and wash them with her tears, and wipe them with the hairs of her head. She said, Christ says, "I love them that love me, and they that seek me early shall find me." But alas! cried she, I have been too long of seeking him: I thought I had been seeking him before; but it was not a right seeking him: so long as I regarded sin in my heart, the Lord did not hear me. I asked her, how she was all night. She said, that after she fell asleep she slept pretty well: she thought somebody was opposing her, and saying, it was not the work of the Lord, which awaked her with this in her mouth, "I will not fear what flesh can do to me," and "O taste and see that God is good!"

She said, that this morning she sung the forty-sixth Psalm, beginning at the 10th verse, and when she came away, she thought it was said to her, "Why weepest thou? Whom seekest thou?" (it is observed that she continued to shed tears abundantly): she said further to me, Worldly thoughts are away from me now, and oh, if they would never return again! Ten thousand worlds could never give me the love and joy which Christ filled me with yesternight, and are not so much as to be compared with them. In the strongest manner she expressed her hatred at sin, and resolutions against it in Christ's strength. And when I put several questions to her, which she satisfactorily answered, she said, Sir, though you put questions to me as was done to Peter, Christ knows my heart, and he who knows all things knoweth that I love him. She said, she resolved to show her love to Christ by keeping his commandments, and that she was sensible her duties were worthless, and can never deserve any thing, but that she had taken Christ's righteousness to be her righteousness in the sight of God. She broke out in surprising words of love and assurance, such as, "He is my sure portion, whom I have chosen for ever." O what hath he done for me when I ruined myself by sin original and actual! Though both my parents have left me, yet the Lord hath taken me up. She said, with great emotion, that she desired to have all the world brought to Christ, and to feel what she felt and doth feel.

June 10th. She told me this day, that she is still under doubts and fears, lest she is too much encouraged; but the following scripture impressed gives her relief: "Let not your heart be troubled; ye believe in God, believe also in me:" And that yesterday when she heard the judgment to come preached upon, she was not afraid of the threatenings, for she saw security in Christ for her; and that she would not be afraid if she saw him coming in the clouds, but that it would be a blessed sight to her, for he was her friend: And that such scriptures as these came into her mind: "Be not afraid, for I am thy God;" and "Why art thou disquieted, O my soul, why art thou cast down within me? Hope still in God; for I shall yet praise him, who is the health of my countenance and my God." She said that she sung the ninety-eighth Psalm with the congregation that day with such joy and comfort as she never could before; and that she might say, as in the fourth Psalm, that she had "more joy than corn and wine" could give her.

Journal from Kilsyth: extracted from my book,
July 20th, 1742

R. S. First touched with convictions upon the Lord's day, May 16th. He heard sermons upon the Wednesday at Kilsyth, and upon the Thursday at Kirkintilloch: but struggled with his convictions untill Thursday night, when he could hold no longer, but, getting up from his father's fireside, ran out to the fields, where he cried out violently under his distress. He came to me on the morning of the 21st of May with great outcries. He had a distressing sight of particular sins, such as Sabbath-breaking, cursing, swearing, evil thoughts. He was grieved for sin as an offence against God, and said with great earnestness, he would give a thousand worlds for Christ.

May 24th. He said, that he saw he had a vile corrupt nature, and the evil of despising Christ through unbelief, and said, he would not for all the world not have had this uneasy sight of sin, or be freed from it untill he come to Christ.

June 8th and 10th. His spiritual distress continuing, and complaining of the hardness of his heart, I endeavoured to instruct him in the nature of faith, and the way of salvation by Jesus Christ.

June 17th. He said, he was very uneasy in the kirk upon Tuesday evening, after he heard the valuable Mr. Whitefield preach that day at Kilsyth. He said, that his heart warmed to Jesus Christ. I asked him, Why? He answered, "Because of his love to poor sinners, and specially to me the chief of all sinners." I enquired at him, if it was accompanied with hatred at sin. He cried out for having offended such a just and holy God, and that he hated every thing that was offensive to him. He said, that he had assayed to close with Christ, and that his very heart warms when he speaks of him; that this word came home to him, and runs continually in his mind: Matt. xi, 28, 29, "Come unto me, all ye that labour and are heavy-laden, and I will give you rest. Take my yoke upon you, and learn of me, for I am meek and lowly in heart: and ye shall find rest unto your souls."

June 24th. He said, he was some easier since he was last with me, and that he had endeavoured to close with a whole Christ, and counts all things but loss and dung for the excellency of the knowledge of Jesus Christ, and that he may win him, and that he hath now an inclination to Christ, and that his heart flutters in him like a bird when he thinks of him.

July 3rd. He told me, that he is now well, for Sabbath last, while a minister was speaking of the prodigal son, and that his father ran to meet him, he thought with himself what a prodigal he had been, and that Jesus Christ had come to him: he was filled with such a sense of it that he was like to flee from the seat where he was sitting. He said, that he was filled with love to Christ from the sense of Christ's love to him; and that he had closed with Christ in all his offices, and laid the stress of his whole salvation upon him, &c. He said to me, "Sir, many a day I have had a light heart in sin; but now my heart is light indeed, and my love to Christ every day grows."

July 13th. He said, that when he was at the Lord's table, to which he was admitted the last Lord's day, he had the greatest comfort in closing with a whole Christ in all his offices, and his heart warmed to him. He had large views of what a vile sinner he had been, and the wonders that grace and mercy had done for him, particularly in bringing him to his holy table. He said, he blessed the Lord with heart and soul and spirit, and all that was within him, for Christ and what he had done for him; and that he had fears lest he should fall away, and made application to Jesus Christ to keep him: and that it was a joyful sight to him when he saw the bread broken, a sign of Christ's body broken for him, which he believed, as also that his blood was shed for him.

I shall add to these other Journals extracted from my book the two following, who neither cried out in public, nor were under bodily distresses.

June 26th. Y. Z. says, he was frequently under concern last winter, while the doctrine of regeneration was preached; and that he examined himself by the scripture marks of regeneration; but could find none of them in himself; yet his concern came no length. He was brought under deeper concern on Sabbath a fortnight past, in hearing the marks of unbelievers in a sermon I preached from John, iii, 36. He says, these cut him wholly off. He was convinced of particular sins, of the evil of unbelief, the corruption of nature, and the need of a new nature. He says, that he is sorry for sin, and would be so though is did not make him liable to hell, because he hath offended and dishonoured God by his sins. As to self-loathing, he saith, that he hates himself for his sins, and is convinced that no sufferings of his can ever satisfy the offended justice of God for the least of his offences, and that if he could abstain from all sin for the time to come, and keep the law perfectly, it could not satisfy for the evil of sin already past; and that this is only to be obtained by the righteousness of Jesus Christ imputed to him. I instructed him in the nature of faith, and pressed him to a distinct acting of it, with a faith and persuasion of his attaining to all that he receives and trusts in Christ for, according to the promise of God.

July 6th. By the account he gives of himself, I am persuaded he hath closed with Christ. I endeavoured to answer and satisfy many objections and doubts he proposed to me: but did not insert them in my book. I advised him to receive the Lord's Supper, but he durst not adventure, being doubtful about his faith and interest in Christ, though he had been formerly a communicant. He hath since attained to some satisfying scriptural marks and evidences of his interest in Christ, hath partaken the Lord's Supper, and continues to walk in the fear of the Lord, and some measure of the comfort of the Holy Ghost.

B. A. came to me, June 18th, and told me, she hath been uneasy since the 16th of May, and that her concern increased upon her on Sabbath, Monday, and Tuesday last. She was convinced of unbelief, and the evil of it;

and was very uneasy about the sin of unworthy communicating; but did not seem to be convinced particularly of her other sins against the law, nor the corruption of her nature, and was sorry for sin only because of its making her liable to the wrath of God. I gave her instructions and directions suitable to the view I had of her case.

July 5th. She then saw particular sins, but was most of uneasy about unworthy communicating, and the evil of unbelief. She professed, that she was sorry for sin, because she had offended God by it, and also that she loathed herself for her sins. She did not as yet appear to be convinced of the corruption of her nature. I advised her to cry to God to convince her of it, to give her faith to embrace Christ as offered to her in the gospel, and that with a dependence upon him she would assay to do it. In all which I endeavoured to instruct her.

July 9th. She said, that she now saw that she brought a corrupt nature with her into the world, that is enmity to God and all good; and that she is lost and undone by it. She said, that she had accepted of Jesus Christ in all his offices, and his righteousness to be hers in the sight of God, seeing all her own righteousness "to be but as filthy rags." She said, that she was much distressed yesterday morning, but was comforted with Isaiah, lxi, 10. After instructions and directions I admitted her to the Lord's table.

July 19th. She said, she was under much fear and terror before she came to the Lord's table, but "I will go in the strength of God the Lord." When she was there she was filled with joy in Christ, as a sufficient Saviour. She had a view of her sins piercing him, and sorrow upon that account; she continues to live and to walk as becometh a good Christian.

D. C. neither cried out in public, nor was she under

99

any bodily distress, though very much distressed inwardly; was with me June 7th, as she had been formerly. She was convinced then of particular sins, the corruption of her nature, and the evil of unbelief. I discoursed with her of the nature of godly sorrow, self-loathing, and pressed her to seek after them, and to plead in prayer, Ezek, xxxvi, 31. She said, that a word came into her mind as strong as if another had spoken it to her, "Draw nigh to God, and he will draw nigh to thee." And at another time, while she was alone and very uneasy, "My heart is fixed, O God, my heart is fixed: I will sing and give praise." I told her these words pointed out to her her duty to draw nigh to God through Jesus Christ, and to seek after a heart fixed and established by grace, to sing and give praise to him.

June 17th and 24th. She told me, both these days, that she was more distressed than formerly, from a distincter view of original sin and corruption than ever she had before. I instructed her, that there was a full and complete relief for her in Christ Jesus from that and all her other sins. She said, it gave comfort to her this last day that this scripture came into her mind: "By his knowledge shall my righteous servant justify many, for he shall bear their iniquities." I told her that the use she should have made of that was, to believe upon Jesus Christ, that she might be justified by faith in him.

About the beginning of July she said, that she had undergone many changes since she was with me. I enquired if she had been endeavouring to embrace Jesus Christ as he was freely offered to her in the gospel. She answered that she was willing to receive him in all his offices, and to part with all things for him; for he is before all things that ever were or shall be; and that she was willing to take Christ's righteousness to be her whole righteousness in the sight of God, renouncing all confi-

100

dence in her works and duties for acceptance before God. She said, that Isa. xlv. 22, and xli. 10, being brought into her mind when she was in great distress, gave her some support. She had great joy while in secret yesterday. The ground of it was a view of Christ's mercy in awakening and coming to so great a sinner, who had grieved his Holy Spirit, and broken all her vows to him: that he might have let her lie still in the Devil's arms, and go to hell; which would have been no loss to him. She said, it was a great pleasure to her to serve such a master, and one who had done so much for her. She further said, that she was uneasy yesterday, about former unworthy communicating, while she was hearing the lecture upon 1 Cor. xi, 23, and that she now mourns for it, and flees to Christ's blood to cleanse her from that guilt. I assured her, that his precious blood, that cleansed these converts mentioned in the second chapter of the Acts from the guilt of this blood, would cleanse her from it if she really did so. She said also, that she endeavoured to obey the gospel call yesterday to close with Christ, and it gave her joy to think of the free access she had to him, and that he would not cast her out. And that yesterday, when she remembered what she heard Mr. Whitefield say of the married man in Matthew xxii, that he should have come and brought his wife with him, she thought that she would come, and if she had ten thousand to bring with her, she would have come with joy to such a Saviour if she could have persuaded them to come.

An Account of the most Remarkable Particulars known to me at the time, concerning the Progress of his Blessed Work.

It is the desire of some, and I hope will be acceptable to many others, to have an account of what shall come to my knowledge of the progress of this work from time to time. This I shall endeavour to give in every print of this Narrative untill it be finished, if the Lord will.

October 3rd. The Lord's Supper was given a second time in this congregation. It was first proposed to me privately by the Rev. Mr. M'Culloch, minister of Cambuslang, when I was there at the giving of the Lord's Supper, August 15th. All I said then was, that I had never thought of it, and that the Lord's Supper was to be given in the neighbouring parish of Cumbernauld after harvest; which appeared to me an objection against any such design. After this I had the proposal much under my consideration, but spoke of it to nobody. Many objections were mustered in my mind against it. I had a rooted aversion at any thing that looked like affecting popularity, and was greatly afraid that the giving the Lord's Supper a second time in the congregation, and within a quarter of a year after it had been given, might be misconstrued this way. While I was thus tossed in my mind, and almost resolved against it, as member of the Session, whose judgment I greatly value, came to me upon a Certain Lord's day betwixt sermons, and proposed it to me as his own desire and also of several others in the congregation, that the sacrament should be given a second time. I was prevailed with to propose it to the Session in the evening. The members of the Session were desired to advertise the several societies for prayer, to seek light and direction from God, to enquire into the sentiments of the people respecting it, and to report to the next Session. After this the Session met again and again, to pray and deliberate about it. I was informed that it was the earnest desire of the generality of the parish to have it. They urged that the Lord had wrought great and extraordinary things in the congregation this summer, in a work of conviction and conversion, and that they thought that the most solemn and extra-ordinary thanksgiving was due to him from them; and which they could not offer to him in a more solemn manner than in this ordinance of thanksgiving. They declared also that they were willing to bear a considerable part of the charges, and offered to bear the whole if it would be accepted. I durst not, after all things considered, refuse to give them the Lord's ordinance, which they had a right to, and so earnestly desired; especially considering that the giving of it at most in country congregations but once a year is a complaint against our constitution. It was resolved then, with an eye to the Lord, to give this ordinance upon the third Sabbath of October.

I was assisted in the giving of it by the neighbouring ministers and former assistants who could be with me; such as the Rev. Mr. M'Laurin, Glasgow, Mr. James Warden, Calder, Mr. John Warden, Campsie, Mr. James Burnside, Kirkintilloch, Mr. James Mackie, St. Ninians, Mr. John Smith, Larbert, Mr. Speirs, Linlithgow, Mr. Thomas Gillespie, Carnock, Mr. Hunter, Saline, Mr. M'Culloch, Cambuslang, and Mr. Porteous, Monivaird. Some of these reverend brethren, who had not been formerly my assistants, were invited to supply the place of some of my neighbours, who could not be with me at this time; or to answer for the more than ordinary demand for preaching and other ministerial work, others of them came to join with us of themselves, and kindly gave their assistance as they were called. Mr. James Young, preacher of the gospel at Falkirk, having been invited, assisted by preaching.

Upon the Fast-day sermon was in the fields to a very numerous and attentive audience, by three ministers without intermission because of the shortness of the day. Upon the Friday evening there was sermon in the kirk, and there was a good deal of concern among the people. Upon the Saturday there was sermon both in the kirk and in the fields.

Upon the Lord's day the public service began about half an hour after eight in the morning, and continued without intermission untill half an hour after eight in the evening, when all was concluded. I preached the action sermon, by the Divine direction and assistance, from Eph. ii, 7, "That in the ages to come he might show the exceeding riches of his grace, in his kindness towards us, through Christ Jesus." There were twenty-two services; each consisting of about seventy persons, except the last, which had only a few, so that the number of communicants amounted to nearly fifteen hundred. The evening sermon began immediately after the last service. And though I desired that the congregation in the fields should be dismissed after the last service, yet they chose rather to continue together untill all was over, when there was the most desirable frame and observable concern among the people that had ever been any where seen; it began to be considerable when the Rev. Mr. Warden, Campsie, preached, and it continued and increased greatly while the Rev. Mr. Speirs preached, who concluded the public work of this day in the fields.

Upon the Monday there were sermons both in the kirk and in the fields. There was a good deal of observable concern and several brought under spiritual distress in the fields. In the evening two ministers had successively public discourses to the numerous distressed convened in the church. As also upon the Tuesday morning there was a sermon preached, and a discourse by another minister, containing suitable instructions and directions, both to the awakened and to them who had never attained to any sense and sight of their sin and danger.

The spiritual fruits of this solemn and extraordinary

dispensation of word and sacrament are, as far as known to me; First: Several Christless and secure sinners were awakened to a sight of their sin and misery, the most of whom were strangers from other congregations at a distance. Zion's mighty King brought the wheel of the law over them, and sent them home with broken and contrite hearts.

Secondly: Some who came here without any sensible relief from the spiritual distress and law-work they had been under for a long time, felt such a time of the Mediator's power as enabled them to embrace Jesus Christ with such distinctness as to know that they had done it; a sovereignly gracious Lord, who comforts them that are cast down, filling them at the same time with such a feeling of his love shed abroad in their hearts by the Holy Ghost given unto them that they could not contain, but were constrained to break forth with floods of tears in their most significant expressions of their own vileness and unworthiness, and of the deep sense they had of the exceeding righes of God's grace in his kindness shown towards them through Jesus Christ.

Thirdly: There were a great many who declared to me, that while they were at the Lord's table, and at other times during this attendance, they had more than ordinary feelings of the love of God to their souls, and outgoings of their love towards the altogether lovely Jesus; and these not only of the elder sort, but some who were very young. A judicious solid Christian told me, that he was so much in this blessed situation that he could scarcely restrain himself from crying out.

There were many strangers from a great distance who came hither to keep this feast to the Lord; several of them of note and distinction in the world, of great penetration and judgment, and long experience in the Christian life, who declared themselves well satisfied with what they had heard, seen, and felt, by the Lord's mercy, in this place, and returned to their houses joyful and glad in heart for the goodness that the Lord had showed unto his people.

I record all this to the praise and glory of our God, in and through Jesus Christ, and that I may mention the loving-kindness of the Lord, and his praises according to all that he hath bestowed on us, and the great goodness towards the house of Israel which he hath bestowed on them according to his mercies and according to the multitude of his loving-kindnesses.

The spiritual fruits of this solemn and extraordinary dispensation of word and sacrament are, as far as known to me; First: Several Christless and secure sinners were awakened to a sight of their sin and misery, the most of whom were strangers from other congregations at a distance. Zion's mighty King brought the wheel of the law over them, and sent them home with broken and contrite hearts.

Secondly: Some who came here without any sensible relief from the spiritual distress and law-work they had been under for a long time, felt such a time of the Mediator's power as enabled them to embrace Jesus Christ with such distinctness as to know that they had done it; a sovereignly gracious Lord, who comforts them that are cast down, filling them at the same time with such a feeling of his love shed abroad in their hearts by the Holy Ghost given unto them that they could not contain, but were constrained to break forth with floods of tears in their most significant expressions of their own vileness and unworthiness, and of the deep sense they had of the exceeding righes of God's grace in his kindness shown towards them through Jesus Christ.

Thirdly: There were a great many who declared to me, that while they were at the Lord's table, and at other times during this attendance, they had more than ordinary feelings of the love of God to their souls, and outgoings of their love towards the altogether lovely Jesus; and these not only of the elder sort, but some who were very young. A judicious solid Christian told me, that he was so much in this blessed situation that he could scarcely restrain himself from crying out.

There were many strangers from a great distance who came hither to keep this feast to the Lord; several of them of note and distinction in the world, of great penetration and judgment, and long experience in the Christian life, who declared themselves well satisfied with what they had heard, seen, and felt, by the Lord's mercy, in this place, and returned to their houses joyful and glad in heart for the goodness that the Lord had showed unto his people.

I record all this to the praise and glory of our God, in and through Jesus Christ, and that I may mention the loving-kindness of the Lord, and his praises according to all that he hath bestowed on us, and the great goodness towards the house of Israel which he hath bestowed on them according to his mercies and according to the multitude of his loving-kindnesses.

Chapter 6

More Visible Scenes

LEARNED and godly Rutherford hath, in the Contents prefixed to his Survey of the Spiritual Antichrist, a title in these words: "The real influence of Spiritual Operations on the Body:" from this I have taken the hint in the terms I have used in this Chapter. The preceding claim all who burst forth into tears and weeping, groaned deeply, or made bitter outcries when they were awakened: This gives the history of those whose bodies were more grievously affected. This I shall endeavour to do with all the faithfullness and openness that becometh an honest man, and with all the distinctness I can attain. The first sort are those who complained of pains in their bodies, namely in their arms and legs, that they were ready, as they expressed it, to break. I have two very strong men in my remembrance while I write this; and they are the only instances I remember. They had been for several hours under distress before I saw them. They had both a distinct and particular conviction of sin because of unbelief, and clear views of the dreadful wrath of God they were under and liable to because of it. The arrows of the Almighty had pierced them to the quick, the poison whereof drank up their spirits. I found that from their awakening they had, in uttering their complaints and fears, and in their frequent and earnest cries to God, wrestled and tossed much with their bodies. To this, as well as to the uncommon earnestness of their minds, I ascribed these pains of their bodies, in their arms, thighs, and legs, that they complained of. I remember one of them said, he had wrestled so that his strength was quite gone. They had been nearly a night and a day in this situation. The Psalmist's words might well be applied to them, "When I kept silence, my bones waxed old, through my roaring all the day long: for day and night thy hand was heavy upon me. My moisture is turned into the drought of summer." Next day their fears were abated, convictions began to do kindly with them, supports and hopes were given by a gracious God, and they complained no more of their bodily pains; yet they attained no sensible abiding relief and comfort for several weeks. They both continue to this 11th of March, 1743, to be knowing, strict, and exemplary Christians.

The second sort are those who were seized with trembling in their bodies when awakened. Of all the bodily effects this was the most frequent. Their bodies would have shaken so that the one nearest to them was necessitated to hold them fast; and sometimes that person came to be awakened, and needed soon another to do the same kindly office to him or her. All of those I conversed with gave still a present sense of their being sinners, and liableness to the wrath of God for sin, less or more distinctly, as the cause of their trembling. So that they might have used the Psalmist's words in some degree, "My flesh trembleth for fear of thee; and I am afraid of thy judgments." I could not miss to think of the scripture instances of Felix's trembling under convictions, which went no further; the very case of too many with us: also of Saul and the jailor trembling when first awakened, which issued in real conversion, as it did with several of ours, through the grace of our God.

A third sort of their fears produced convulsive-like motions in some men or boys, and what I took to be hysteric fits in women or girls. There were but very few men who were thus affected; not above three or four that I can remember: in none of them they came to such a height as to deprive them of their judgment and senses for any time: and they were all men of weak spirits and bodily constitutions, and but small measure of knowledge. There were about half a dozen of boys, in whom also convulsive motions appeared to come to a greater height, and to make them insensible for some time. There were also some few women and several young girls who were seized with such fits whenever their thoughts about their sinful lost state, and being without God and Christ, increased their fears to a great height. I observed as to them likewise, that some of them were very ignorant; others, though they had some notional knowledge, yet had no distinct view of the sinner's way of relief by Jesus Christ. And others again were of tender and weakly constitutions, and possibly have been under some degree of hysteric fits formerly. A good many of these, who were diligent in the use of means, came by the power of God's grace to a good and comfortable issue, or are in a hopeful way. Several who were grossly ignorant did not apply themselves with a patient diligence in the use of means to get knowledge, and their general convictions of a sinful state and fears came to nothing. These convulsive effects prejudiced many of the common sort against this blessed work. They know no other convulsions but the epilepsy, or what they call the falling-sickness. They know not that there are many sorts of convulsions which are not the falling-sickness, or the fits, another name ordinary among them; and therefore whatever they hear called convulsions, hysteric fits, &c., they understand in the

110

worst sense, for the falling-sickness, which they have great dread for. Some of the seceding ministers knowing this prejudice and weakness of the vulgar have, without the least shadow of truth, represented this at a distance in the worst shape, as epilepsies, and accompanied with foamings and other epileptic symptoms, whereas, as far as I could either observe or hear, there was not one who was seized with epilepsy or falling-sickness, or foamed: but some opposers have forged it, as it is well known they have done many other things. And as I have known no instance of the epilepsy, so it is worthy of observation that there is no instance wherein any of these troubles became periodical with any of them, though they recurred frequently upon them before their fears were removed. Some of those women appeared to faint in these hystericisms, and could not speak, but yet heard and understood what was said to them: And the spirit of sal-ammoniac or hartshorn put to their noses was useful to revive them. Their pulse was not much disordered. Others neither heard nor were otherwise sensible; spirits put to their noses had little influence upon them: their pulse was disordered and their colour changed. There were also some who fainted and fell over as dead without any unusual motion upon their bodies. All these gave the inward fears of their souls as the cause of the disorder of their bodies, and the ground and reason of their fears their being convinced and made sensible in a way they never were before that they were sinners.

Those of the third class were but few compared with the number of the other sorts of the awakened. The reader may judge by this one instance. Upon the 16th of May, when there were nearly thirty awakened, and known to me that night, there was not one of these in the third class mentioned that I can remember, or any other I have enquired at. And yet it is worth notice, that in proportion to this number, as many of this third as of any other class were, through the tender mercy of the Most High, brought to a good issue; there was only one of this sort whom I discovered to be like those in Lochlairn. The disorder of her body appeared to me more affected than natural: she was very easy-like in her aspect when she came out of it: she was grossly ignorant, and I could find in her no distinct sight and sense of sin; and though she was at pains for a few weeks to learn to read, yet she gave it over. I charged her not to be any more so affected in her body when she was hearing the word; which had the effect that she never appeared so afterwards, and she continuous stupid, careless, and ignorant as formerly. Possibly there might be some others of this same sort who, being thus affected, came to me once or twice, and I heard no more of them — this being a case that could not be counterfeited for any time.

There have also been instances here, of those on whom the joys and comforts of the Holy Ghost have had sensible influence. Some who had been under deep apprehensions of Divine wrath, and sunk under a sense of their guilt, when the Lord enlightened their minds in the knowledge of Christ, opened their hearts to receive him as offered to them in the gospel, so explicitly and expressly as to know they had done it: and at the same time had views of the exceeding riches of his grace, of the glory of Jesus Christ, and of his ability and willingness to save them: They have been surprised with such measures of joy and admiration as have made their hearts to leap; some to cry out with a loud voice, expressing their admiration, and showing forth the praises of the Lord; others also to break forth into loud weeping, with a flood of tears from a sense of their own unworthiness and vileness; some have had their bodies quite overcome for a time, and ready if not actually to faint through the feeling of such unexpected comforts and joys. I have seen those who have had their countenance quite changed. An observable serenity, brightness, and openness was and continued upon their face. So that it was the observation of some concerning them, that they had got new faces: the Lord's countenance hath been also the health of some, recovering them from long weakness and bodily distress.

Under this Chapter an historical account is to be given of those whose imaginations appeared to have been affected. There have been exceedingly great misrepresentations of this both here and elsewhere. The instances of such are very few, and so inconsiderable that they gave no manner of uneasiness. Very near the beginning of this work, I instructed the congregation, by the help of grace, in the strongest, plainest, and most express manner I could, that Jesus Christ in the body cannot be seen by any with their bodily eyes in this life; "For the heavens must receive him untill the times of the restitution of all things:" — That such a sight of him, if it were attainable, would not save them; seeing many had it in the days of his flesh who yet continued and perished in their unbelief, and therefore if any of them should afterwards think they got any such sights, they would be well persuaded that it was owing only to the strength of their imagination, to the disorder of their head, and of the humours of their bodies at that time, and that it was not real; and that they would especially guard against building any hope upon it, or thinking that their case was bettered by it. This possibly might be one reason why there was so little of this to be observed here. I found none who appeared to have had impressions upon their imaginations but were ready to receive instruction, and easily persuaded that no weight was to be laid upon any of these things. This made me easy and not much alarmed with the few instances I met with or heard of this kind; especially considering that they evidently appeared to be the natural result, in some constitutions, of the earnestness of their mind and some present disorder of their bodies, and as I was far from looking upon these things as any part of the work of the Spirit, or any sign of it; so I was as far from looking upon them as inconsistent and incompatible with it. I had read and known so many instances of these things ere now that I was in no danger of either. In one of the spring months, before there was any appearance of this work, I met with a remarkable instance of this kind, which was afterwards considerably useful to me. It was in a man who had been a Christian of considerable standing, and of good repute for understanding, profession, and practice, who was sick for some months, of which sickness he afterwards died. At a time when I visited him, he said there was something he wanted to enquire at me and be satisfied about. I assured him I was ready to satisfy him what I could. He said, that some days before that he had been much in earnest and serious prayer or meditation; he thought he saw our Lord Jesus Christ as he hung upon the cross — the wounds in his hands and feet, and the blood running from his precious wounds. His affections had been greatly moved, as they were also when he repeated the story to me, and enquired at me what he should think of it. I instructed him as I best could, that he could see no such things by his bodily eyes: that it was owing merely to his being much affected in his thinking upon the death of Jesus Christ, to the strength of his imagination, and to the present bad habit of his body; that it was another sight of Jesus Christ as he was pierced that he was to seek after and be exercised in, namely, that mentioned in Zech. xii, 10. This I am persuaded he had attained before that, at that time, and afterwards.

This the honest man was convinced of and satisfied with. It never entered into my mind to assign it to the Devil, seeing I could find a sufficient cause for it in the man himself; much less to conclude it inconsistent with a work of grace upon the good man, especially seeing he laid no weight upon it, wanted to be instructed what to judge of it, and readily received instruction; so that if I had seen any of the awakened who had been in this honest man's situation it would have given me no manner of fear or uneasiness about them. There is nothing I know here that came this length.

I shall give a faithful history of all I can certainly remember or have recorded relative to this subject.

Of the many hundreds I have conversed with, there is only one who said she thought she saw hell open as a pit to receive her, one time while she was standing upon the stair that leads to my closet; and this was nearly a month after her first awakening. I told her it was owing to her imagination, and that she must see the wrath of God due to her for her sins in the threatening of the law. Her convictions made but slow progress, yet at length they appeared to have come to a desirable issue; and she continues, by what I hear, to behave as becometh a Christian. It is to be observed, that her awakening began with her being convinced that she was in a Christless state, and of the sadness of such a state.

There were none who ever said to me, that they thought they saw the blessed Jesus in any form. I heard indeed of three, a woman and two girls, who at one particular time, after much distress of body and mind, said to those with them, that they saw Jesus Christ: but I met with them afterwards, and examined into it, and they appeared to be ashamed of it, and were convinced that they had really seen nothing. And they did not love to speak of it, they were so far from building any good hope upon it: and by what I could find, those about them, and report from hand to hand, had aggravated things much: however the woman hath all the evidences can be desired of her being a tender Christian, though at the same time of a weak head; and both the girls are most hopeful.

There were three women who said to me, that once, when they were under deep concern and great earnestness, they thought they saw a great and glorious light for a very short time. But when I examined into the circumstances, I found that their eyes had been shut at the time, and so easily convinced them that it was not real but imaginary, and that no weight was to be laid upon it by them. These three are likewise promising and hopeful.

I had a few instances, who alleged that they had been frightened with the appearance of the Devil; but when I examined narrowly into it, I could find no further reason for it than their legal and slavish fears, under a conviction of God's being their enemy, and that of all his creatures, because of their sins, which were set in order before their eyes. What in some of these instances they apprehended to be the Devil, seemed to be no more than some dog that came in their way in the night-time, while they were going to pray or had been praying in some solitary place. It did not appear strange to me, to find a few instances (within six) among country people who are from their infancy bred up with stories about frightful appearances, especially in their present situation, when the arrows of the Almighty were within them, the poison whereof drank up their spirits, and the terrors of God did set themselves in array against them, Job, vi, 4. It gave me some pleasure to observe, that no fright of that kind could drive them from their prayers.

That I may conceal nothing — a judicious young man,

and whose convictions seemed to issue in real conversion, having used to go in the night-time to his father's barn and continue there in prayer for some considerable time, said he was frequently disturbed with a noise, as if the roof of the house would have come down upon him. I assigned all the ordinary causes for it I could possibly think upon; but he affirmed it could be none of these: he still kept to the place, though it continued for the most part of several weeks. A young woman, of a good character from her infancy, and upon whom I hope a saving change hath been wrought last summer, some little before this signal appearance of God in this congregation dreamed, that a man came to warn all the people about the town that the Lord was coming; and the warning was given in the words of Micah, "The Lord's voice crieth unto the city, and the man of wisdom shall see thy name. Hear ye the rod and who hath appointed it," — telling her chapter and verse: Also in the words of Isa. lviii, 1, "Cry aloud, spare not, lift up thy voice like a trumpet, and show my people their transgressions, and the house of Jacob their sins." Upon this she awakened and ran to her bible, and was surprised to find chapter and verse answer exactly to what she had dreamed. She professed she had no occasion to notice particularly these scriptures before; and knew not untill she looked into her bible that they were as she had dreamed. There are some few instances of persons who have in their sleep been directed to scriptures exactly suited to the present case of their souls.

I shall conclude this Chapter with an account of this good work in congregations to the northward of Glasgow, since October last.

The observable state of things in this congregation, during the months of November, December and January, was, that those who had been awakened, but

117

had attained to no desirable outgate, continued to make progress, and to profit by the use of the outward and ordinary means of grace, especially to the younger sort, whose progress was very sensible. They who appeared to have received the Lord Jesus Christ continued to all outward appearance to walk in him, and to grow in grace and in the knowledge of our Lord Jesus Christ, as they continue through grace to do unto this day, March 26th, 1743. There are not above two or three of them known to me whom I have had reason to rebuke for any thing amiss in their walk. Many of them came frequently to me these months, and since, with fears and doubts about their spiritual state: some of their doubts and fears arose from their feeling vanity of mind, wandering of their hearts in the time of holy duties, evil thoughts, hardness of heart, and other inward corruptions; so that they complained that they were worse and wickeder than ever they found themselves to be before, not considering that formerly they were dead, but now they had life and feeling: that formerly they were darkness, and now they were light in the Lord. Others complained of their want of love to Christ, and of spiritual deadness, because lively motions of their affections were abated. Some of these wanted to know by what marks and signs they might know that they loved our Lord Jesus Christ in sincerity. Others were afraid, and jealous that their faith might not be of the right sort, and lest they should deceive themselves. Many of them complained much of atheistical thoughts, blasphemous injections, as it were inward dissuasions from prayer and other holy duties, and other sorts of the fiery darts of the wicked one. The societies for prayer continued and increased, so that at present they are above twenty-two, which meet once in the fortnight, once in the week, and some of them oftener. The outward reformation of the congregation continues. And during these months mentioned there was great diligence in attendance upon gospel ordinances, and great appearance of seriousness and concern in hearing, without any considerable outcry. There were few or none newly awakened known to me these months, though I find since that there were some, who had concealed themselves for a time; only there were some few in and about the town of Kilsyth, then and since, to the number of twenty-three, who of themselves associated for prayer. I hope it shall issue well with some of them, through the tender mercy of the Most High, though there are grounds of fear as to others of them.

Since the beginning of February the operations of the Holy Spirit have been again more sensible, both as to the awakening of secure sinners, and reviving those formerly converted. All or most of the societies of the congregation set apart Tuesday the eighth of February, for thanksgiving to the God and Father of our Lord Jesus Christ, for this surprising and unlooked-for appearance of his grace in so many congregations of this backslidden church and land, and for prayer that it may be general through the length and breadth of the land. There was also transmitted to us, a memorial from the societies for prayer at Edinburgh, inviting the praying societies in this congregation and the congregations about, to join with them, upon the 18th day of February, in thanksgiving and prayer to God upon the foresaid account.

This congregation kept the same day congregationally. The Rev. Mr. Spears, minister of Linlithgow, assisting me in the public work, when there was a very great concern in the congregation. And Mr. Spears and I had much to do in the evening, in conversing with those under distress who had as yet got no outgate; as also with several of those who had got an escape through grace, but were under great distress at the time, through various temptations. The societies for prayer met at night; the societies in the congregations about kept this day, or some part of it. The minister of Kirkintilloch preached upon the Thursday, being the 17th, and I think the societies of that parish met upon the same day.

I remark this more particularly, to manifest and set forth the glory and praise of our God, who is the hearer of prayer, and who hath been gracious to us at the voice of our cry, for his Son, and for his holy name's sake. The month of February has been the most remarkable month for the presence of the Lord among us, not only in this congregation but some others about, of any since October last. From Sabbath the thirteenth to Sabbath the twentieth of February there were ten awakened either altogether new, or such upon whom their first awakening had long since come to nothing; since which there have been about eight with me, most of them under fourteen. All this besides thirteen young boys, who had associated themselves for prayer, without any desiring them, and who are since taken under such notice as is needful for them. Last month and this hath also been a time of reviving, strengthening, and confirming to former Christians, and of relieving some of the late converts from their distresses. Of all this I have good documents, some of which shall be given upon the article of reviving in this Narrative, if the Lord permit.

There are at this time nearly seventy, if not above, from eight to eighteen years of age or thereby, most of whom meet in societies twice a week, and spend the time in prayer, singing some part of a psalm, reading the Scriptures, and repeating their catechism. They are at least once a week under the inspection and direction of some elder Christian who meets with them.

Journal from Kilsyth, sent by a letter from the Minister,
June 9th, 1742.

E. F., about twenty-five years of age, blameless in his former life, and professing religion, began to be convinced more than ordinarily about his spiritual state, from the day he heard the Rev. Mr. Willison of Dundee preach here about the 23rd of April. This concern increased the Lord's day thereafter, upon his seeing a young girl awakened and fainting in the congregation. He says, that he reasoned thus within himself, that when a girl so young was so deeply affected with a sense of her sin and danger, his case was sad, who was so little affected.

Upon the Lord's day, being the 16th of May, when there were many brought into spiritual distress, his anxiety about his soul greatly increased.

Monday morning he went to a sheep-cote for prayer. By the way he was much concerned, fearing that the Lord had passed him by, and earnestly desiring that the Holy Spirit might come for his conviction and awakening. As soon as he came thither and bowed his knees to prayer, he said, "O mighty God of Jacob, why passest thou by me? send thy Holy Spirit to convince and awaken me, and give me a discovery of myself." Upon which he fell into great distress, seeing himself lost and undone, and thought he got a sight of all his sins, both original and actual, and that so particularly that he could confess them by name unto the Lord. He says, that his particular sins came continually into his mind one after another; and that he could not leave the place without confessing them to the Lord: which kept him from eight till ten in the morning. He says further, that he saw the dreadful evil of unbelief, and was made to cry out against it as a damnable sin; and broke out in thankfulness to

God for awakening him, and thought it was so great a mercy, that he could not be thankful enough for it, nor could he, as he says, get the greatness of the mercy out of his mind. He was brought to me the same day, under the greatest agonies of any I have seen. Upon the 18th of May, his case appeared to me very hopeful, and continued so in his coming to me from time to time.

May 31st, he told me he was grieved for sin, because offensive to God, but thinks he cannot get grief enough for his sins. I told him, if he had such a sense of sin, and degree of humiliation, as made him willing to part with all sin, that was the measure to be desired. He said, that he was afraid lest there be yet some sin that he is not willing to part with, that the Lord doth not send relief to him. I told him it was too much of a legal spirit to expect relief upon the account of any thing attained by him; and that he must look for it upon Christ's account, and wait patiently the Lord's time, who is sovereign in giving comfort as well as grace; and that he must search and try whether there be not some sin he is not willing to part with, and which, if he did not, would separate between God and him. He said, worldliness was a dreadful sin, and frequently came into his mind in duty. I advised him to humble himself before God for it, and to cry to him to search and try him, and to see every wicked way in him. He said, he desired to part with that and all other sin.

I asked him what views he had of Christ. He said he saw him to be an all-sufficient Saviour, able and willing "to save to the uttermost;" but that all the fault was in his own unwillingness; and that he assayed frequently to close with Jesus Christ. I asked him what he took closing with Christ to be. He answered, that he took closing with Christ to be a receiving him as a Prophet to teach him the way of salvation, as a Priest to atone for him and to be his righteousness in the sight of God, and as a King to rule over him and to subdue sin and corruption in him; and that without Christ's righteousness imputed to him he can never be accepted in the sight of God. I told him, he must also rely upon Jesus Christ for salvation, with some confidence and persuasion of faith, to obtain it according to the promise. He said, that it was there where it struck with him. I advised him to go and mourn for this unbelief, and to pray for the spirit of faith, and to assay this way of believing.

June 4th, he came to tell me that he had gotten sensible relief. He said, that upon Wednesday, June 2nd, in hearing the sermon upon the Spirit's convincing the world of righteousness, from John, xvi, 10, he had considerable satisfaction: he was made to see the insufficiency of his own righteousness, and the sufficiency of Christ's, and that he could not be justified in the sight of God without it, and was willing to disclaim his own and accept of Christ's He told me further, that coming to hear sermon upon the said Wednesday, his master by the road told him several marks of grace, which he thought he could find in himself: namely, hatred at all sin, because contrary to God; love to the people of God, as the people of God; and an earnest desire to have all others brought to Christ, especially his relations; and that he went home meditating upon the sermon.

Next day, namely, June 3rd, one I know to have been a good Christian a long time, and of the best memory I have known, was with him the most part of the forenoon, and repeated to him, at his desire, all the heads of the foresaid sermon several times over, and prayed with him. In the afternoon he went to a barn and assayed to close with Christ, which he was enabled to do with distinctness, where he got such clearness as not to doubt of his interest in him, and broke out in the high praises of God. He was refreshed with the following scripture: "Behold I stand at the door and knock; if any man hear my voice, and open the door, I will come in to him, and will sup with him, and he with me." He sought and found it out, and in reading over the third chapter of the Revelation, where it is, he was filled with wonder at the greatness of God's grace in bestowing such privileges upon and exalting man after this sort; and his heart was filled with such joy and love to Christ, that he was like to leap off the seat where he was sitting. He says, that he was much affected in reading the 12th verse of the said chapter, ad that he could scarcely believe that it was so with him: wherein he was like unto the disciples "who believed not for joy," but wondered, when they had a risen Jesus among them. He was directed to the seventy-first Psalm, in the words whereof he praised God, and said, he could not end untill he sung the last line of the 6th verse, "I ever will praise thee." He said, he was afraid lest he should fall back again into worldliness, and be ensnared by bad company. I told him he must say and do as David did, "Depart from me, ye evil-doers; for I will keep the commandments of my God.

JAMES ROBE.

Journal from Kilsyth: Extracted from my book,
June 30th, 1742

L. M., aged about twenty-eight years, and formerly of a blameless life, was awakened on May 17th, by seeing and conversing with his brother under spiritual distress. On the night of the 17th he was so deeply distressed that he could sleep very little, but was like one distracted with terrors. Next morning his distress was encreased by reading that passage of Alleine's Alarm wherein he discourseth of God's being an enemy to unconverted sinners; which passage he met with at the first opening of the book.

May 18th, He was brought to me under great agonies affecting his body though a very strong man. I observed his reason clear and undisturbed, and that he gave a distinct account of himself. He was exercised with a view of particular sins, and in a lively manner felt himself to be a guilty condemned sinner; had a deep impression of original sin and corruption as rendering him liable to eternal wrath, though he had not been guilty of any actual sin; had a deep sense of the sinfulness of sin as done against God, and of the sin of unbelief as hardening his heart against the voice of Christ in reading and hearing his word: he was struck with the dreadful fears of falling into the state of torment; and saw the great goodness and long-suffering of God in not cutting him off in the act of some sin or other. He was supported somewhat with the views of the remedy Christ Jesus, and that he came into the world to save sinners, which he desired to lay hold on for the ground of his hope. After this day he conversed with me and some other ministers several times.

May 20th, He seemed to have attained to some composure by assaying to close with Jesus Christ.

May 28th, He declared that when he was engaged in prayer, he felt his soul going out in the acceptance of a whole Christ as his only Saviour, in all his offices for his salvation: his Prophet to teach him by his word and Spirit; his Priest to reconcile him to God by his sacrifice; and his King to subdue his sin, sanctify, and rule him; disclaiming all confidence in his duties and desiring to rely on him alone for salvation; withall giving away himself to the Lord to be saved upon his own terms, to live unto him and serve him in newness of life; resolving, in the strength of Jesus Christ, to live a holy life to his glory, and yet not to rest on it as a ground of peace and acceptance. He said, he was greatly afraid lest he should fall back into sin and be a scandal on religion, after what God had done for him; and that he was exercised with the fears of hypocrisy and presumption in receiving Christ, against which it relieved him to look to Christ anew, who came to save the chief of sinners, and is offered to him in common with others.

June 26th, He told me, that after some new awakenings he had attained to greater degrees of sensible relief. Particularly the reading of the Rev. Mr. Whitefield's text, Mark, xvi, 16, in the congregation, struck him to the heart, and he cried, "Lord, I believe, help my unbelief:" after which, during a good part of the sermon, he endeavoured to close with Christ in all his offices, and was filled with wonder at the grace of God, who had done such wonderful things for him, a poor miserable blind and naked sinner. He got over all his former doubts and fears; had great stirrings of love to Christ: and could not tell what way to praise God, wishing that all the saints would praise him, for he could not do it enough, "Christ was once offered to bear the sins of many; and unto them that look for him will he appear the second time without sin unto salvation," was brought to him in great light, and he had some views of the glory and excellency of Christ and of his love to him. That night his lively frame went off for three days; but yet he was without doubts and fears.

Friday night, as he says, he attained to a lively frame, and observed that the Holy Spirit had set all his affections astirring, and warmed them after Christ, as he terms it.

Saturday morning, he found himself loaded with spiritual joy, and when he went to prayer many promises were brought home to him; he saw them to be "Yea and amen in Christ Jesus," and that they not only belonged to him, but had what he calls a heart-feeling of them. He says, he had a great sense of Christ's love to him, and was filled with joy. This frame continued with him through the day. In the evening, reading the seventh and eighth chapters of the Romans, he thought he had a heart-feeling of every thing in them,. and as he says, he could not apply one promise by another, for he thought that all belonged to him. And that he hath the grounded faith and persuasion of the eighth chapter of the Romans from the 35th verse to the end. He said further, that his case and exercise were an allusion, as he called it, to the men at sea mentioned in Psalm cvii, from the 23rd to the 28th verse, which he read to me.

The above persons, as they were blameless in their lives before, are now spiritual and edifying in their ordinary converse, and exemplary in their conversation; and their lives have been unexceptionable, edifying, and christianly useful, to this 21st of April.

JAMES ROBE.

Seventh Journal from Kilsyth, extracted from my Book, July 7th, 1742.

N. O. came to me under much trouble of mind, June 2nd. He told me he found himself first affected upon the 19th of May, while he was hearing the word of God preached in this congregation, and that his spiritual distress has continued to increase upon him, and that many particular sins he hath done stare him in the face and make him uneasy, and that he can name them to God in confession when he prays.

June 3rd. He told me that his sight of particular sins is encreasing, and that he is convinced he hath been in a state of unbelief all his life, and that it is a dreadful sin, and further, that he sees the corruption of his nature to be such that unless it be taken away from him he cannot be healed or saved. He said that he was born an heir of hell, and was under the wrath of God and condemning sentence of his law also, because of his actual transgressions. I enquired at him the reason why he was sorry for his sins: he answered, because the justice of God threatened him in the word with wrath for sin, and that he could not be saved unless he was sorry for his sins. I instructed him that he must be sorry for his sins because he had offended a just, holy, merciful, and gracious God by them, and that this must be the chief and principal reason of his sorrow for sin, else it would not be godly sorrow, working repentance unto salvation, never to be repented of, and that the other, which was only sorrow for sin because of wrath, though reasonable and allowed, yet it was but legal and selfish where there was no more.

June 7th, He was with me, and declared that he was sorry for his sins because he had offended God by them, and that he had never done any duty acceptably, though there is no dependence upon duties for acceptance with God when done. I asked him, what use he endeavoured to make of hearing yesterday the dreadful misery unbelievers are under and liable to because of unbelief preached: he answered, he endeavoured to do as the prodigal did, to return to his Father's house, to lay aside his unbelief, and to believe upon the Lord Jesus Christ; I instructed him then, as I had done formerly, in the nature of faith, and pressed it upon him.

June 17th, He said, that since he had been with me, he had been more distressed than ever; for Saturday night last he read a sermon of Mr. Andrew Gray upon "praying without ceasing," and finding himself come so far short of what he saw in that sermon, he fell into a swoon, and lay a long time insensible, and that of all his other sins his unbelief most affected him.

June 28th, He said, that he had now great joy because he could mourn much for unbelief, and endeavoured to lay it aside. He said that at Calder he was enabled distinctly to accept of Jesus Christ, which was followed with such joy that he thought if he had the tongues of all the angels in heaven and men upon the earth, he would not get enough of praise to God; and that for the most part of that night he was employed in prayer and praise. He was cast down upon the Thursday because of felt unbelief, but upon the Wednesday he was brought again to a comforted frame by the blessing of the Lord upon some things he heard spoken from Psalm cxxxviii, before the singing of it in the congregation. He was with me this day, and continues to believe upon the Lord Jesus Christ with peace and joy.

JAMES ROBE.

Chapter 7

Across All Frontiers

THE work of God's Spirit, which is the subject of this Narrative, as to its extent hath not been confined to one sort of persons, but hath been extended to some of every denomination and kind.

Those who have been the subjects of the awakening, and, I am persuaded, also of the regenerating influences of the Holy Spirit, have been of all ages.

Many solid divines are of opinion that there are but few of those who live under the gospel from their infancy who are converted after they are thirty years of age. And, indeed, for some number of years past, it hath been rarely heard of before this present time, that any number were converted after middle age. This should excite all persons under that age speedily and earnestly to seek after grace and to come to Christ, lest either they be cut off by death in their youth, and so their life be eternally among the unclean, or enter into that period of life wherein the conversion of sinners is rarer than in that wherein they are. But at the time that we write of there were many persons past middle-age, even as far as hoary hairs, that were awakened; and of these a goodly number converted. The greatest part of them between thirty and forty years of age; a few between forty and fifty; much like the same number between fifty and sixty;

not above two or three above sixty; only one near or above eighty. I speak of those known to me in this parish or neighbourhood. I can say no great things of these old persons beyond awakening, and a professed serious concern to learn the way of salvation by Jesus Christ; so great was their ignorance, the weakness of their faculties, and the confusion either of their ideas or want of words to express them. As this is an express warning to every young reader, I entreat thee to stop a little and think upon it if thou be such a one, not to delay conversion and turning to God by Jesus Christ untill the shadows after mid-day lengthen upon them; so the instances given, joined with the calls and promises of the gospel, serve greatly to give hope and encouragement to the oldest Christless sinner to return to God by faith in Jesus Christ. You who read this, being old and yet unconverted, have indeed great reason to be ashamed that so many young ones have got the start of you; but you have no reason to forbear a diligent use of means to be converted, from a despair of attaining it when you are old or of finding mercy in case you shall be converted. The comparatively fewer instances of people converted after middle age than of those before it should excite the greater diligence, but by no means should take away hope to succeed, seeing there are instances. Say not, old sinner, as Nicodemus, "Shall a man return into his mother's womb, being old?" Regeneration is a spiritual work, and you are capable of it though you are old. God promiseth to pour out his Spirit upon old ones, Acts, ii, 17. He can raise up to himself a temple from a ruinous heap of stones that is ready to drop in pieces. Let not therefore the greater difficulties of conversion in your age weaken your hands; let them rather quicken you to strive with greater earnestness to attain that which others, with all your disadvantages, have notwithstanding attained.

There were a very considerable number of young men and women from twenty to thirty years of age, awakened and hopefully converted; and also, I trust, they are by grace this day "strong, have the word of God abiding in them, and by faith overcome the wicked one." I am persuaded, that if the awakened of this period are compared with the awakened either under or above it, it may be found that fewer of them in proportion have miscarried or failed of the grace of God than of those others.

There have been not a few under twenty years of age awakened, and several of them savingly wrought upon. "Out of the mouths of babes and little children God hath ordained to himself praise, to still the enemy and the avenger." One of six years of age was awakened; she was in great distress, and cried out much when she was first awakened. When she was brought to me after sermon, I was greatly surprised with such an instance. I enquired at her wherefore she cried, and what ailed her: She answered, Sin. I asked her how she came to feel that sin ailed her: she answered, "From the preaching." I asked her what she had heard in the preaching that so much affected her: she answered, "She heard me say, that they who got not an interest in Christ would go to hell." And she said that she would fain have an interest in him. This was upon the 23rd of June, 1742. Upon the 27th of June, being the Lord's-day, she was greatly distressed during the whole time of the sermon. Among other things I asked her at night, what she would give for an interest in Christ: she answered that she would give her life for Christ. July 6, Her distress continuing, she was again with me: she said, that it was sin ailed her; for it deserved God's wrath and curse both in this life and in that which is to come. She was brought to me from time to time untill winter, and I instructed her as the Lord enabled me. I enquired at her if she know any sins in particular she had done against God: she answered, "Lying and banning." "She frequently told me, in answer to such questions, that she prayed most of all to get an interest in Christ; and that she wanted to get Christ to save her from her sins; and that she was willing to have him to be her Saviour. Her parents went out of the parish to some distance, and I have not heard of her for some years past. There was another of seven years of age awakened the same summer; she lived near me and came often to me; she attained to a good measure of knowledge; she was a member of one of the meetings of the young ones: and, as I was informed, she prayed far beyond what could have been expected from her age. She is since deceased: she died professing to be sensible of her need of Christ.

There were above seventy from nine to seventeen or eighteen years of age awakened. There were some of these who at length lost the impressions made upon them, and their convictions in time came to nothing. There are above forty of them who, after long instruction, and a profession of their acceptance of the Lord Jesus Christ as their Saviour, and of God in him for their chief good and last end, have been admitted to the Lord's table frequently; and, by what I can know of them, walk as becometh the gospel. Some of these were awakened at ten, eleven, and twelve years of age; they gave hopeful evidences of a saving change, and continue so to do. I could give a particular account of the progress of the work of God upon their souls, from the Journal that I kept, as has been done in the preceding part of this Narrative, but forbear, lest I increase the bulk of this book.

It is an observation of practical writers, that there are no sort of sinners excepting one that Christ, in a way of saving grace, does not call some of effectually to himself; so it was in this place. There were several, who had made some profession of religion, and were blameless in their lives, who were at this time greatly awakened and thoroughly convinced of their being Christless unbelievers; and a work of conversion was hopefully carried on upon them. There were also several who had been guilty of gross sin, such as adulterers, cursers and swearers, drunkards, and dishonest persons, who were greatly awakened; and some of these gave ground to hope their saving conversion; and that it might be said to them, what the apostle saith to the Corinthians, "And such were some of you, but ye are washed, but ye are sanctified, but ye are justified, in the name of the Lord Jesus and by the Spirit of our God." There were some of good knowledge and understanding who were awakened and convinced, that they knew nothing yet as they ought to know; and willingly became fools, that they might be spiritually and really wise: "counting all things but loss for the excellency of the knowledge of Jesus Christ our Lord." There were some grossly ignorant persons also awakened, who were at little pains to get knowledge, and make proficiency therein; and there is good ground to hope well; of some of them, even "that God who made the light to shine out of darkness, shined into their hearts, to give unto them the light of the knowledge of his glory in the face of Jesus Christ."

There were many men awakened, and to appearance, savingly changed, as well as many women. There were many of strong, courageous, and stout spirits, as well as some of timorous and weak minds and spirits, who were subdued to Christ in this the day of his power. There were many of healthy bodies and constitutions who were made sensible of their spiritual sickness; and of their need of Jesus Christ the Physician of souls, and whom he both wounded and healed: and there were also a few of melancholic and hysteric dispositions who were healed by Christ's stripes; and there is nothing of what is called religious melancholy remaining with them, as far as is known to me. I know no instance here of any persons whose bodily health or understandings have been hurt by the most violent effects of their awakening; but, since the ceasing of their awakenings, either in a right or in a wrong way, they have been as healthy as before. Yea, there is an instance of a young woman who had been for some years under a wasting and consumptive distemper, keeping her bed for the most part, who obliged her friends to carry her one evening to hear God's word, where she was awakened. She was so low that I thought she would live but a few days; yet from that time she recovered, and in appearance the Lord made both her soul and body whole.

It would run too far to be more particular; neither do I find it advisable to enter upon other Articles proposed in the beginning of this Narrative: I shall therefore proceed to the conclusion of it.

Chapter 8

Persevering

THERE were many, in the years 1742 and 1743, while we had the desirable days of the Son of man in this and other congregations, who called upon us not to be too hasty in pronouncing the then extraordinary work to be good until we saw the fruits of it in the after lives and conversations of those who were the subjects of it; and who asserted, that we could affirm nothing of the conversion of such persons until it was manifested by persevering in goodness for some time. I do not remember that I ever heard such persons condescend on how many years such subjects were to be continued under trial ere we could warrantably entertain and declare such a charitable persuasion of a good work being begun and carrying on in them, as one Christian may have of another. They have never hitherto told us whether this time of probation was to extend to two, three, four, or nine years, or untill the death of the subjects of this good work. I have formerly, in my Monthly History for the years 1743, &c., testified to the public the continuance of many of them in such a way as "showed their faith by their works." I published also in that history the express declaration of others, testifying the same concerning those within their knowledge: particularly a long accurate letter from the Rev. Mr.

Warden, then minister of Campsie, but now at Perth, dated December 16th, 1743.

I am now to conclude my Narrative of this extra-ordinary work at Kilsyth, &c., with this Chapter concerning the perseverance of those who appeared to be converted in this and other parishes of the neighbour-hood, in the years 1742 and 1743. It hath been long delayed, and, in the opinion of several who often called upon me to finish it with such an Article, is too long. This delay was partly owing to design and partly to other reasons needless to insert here.

This Chapter comes now to be published more season-ably than it could have been any time before this. The false and malicious reports spread in several places in Scotland, at a distance from this, Cambuslang, &c., that this extraordinary work was come to nought, and that all the subjects of it were turned worse and wickeder than they were before, were sufficiently contradicted by what I published in the Monthly History.

We are greatly rejoiced, and excited to praise the God of all grace, by accounts we have had from Holland of such an extraordinary work of the Holy Spirit being begun at Niewkerk, Putten, &c., in the Duchy of Guelderland, about the latter end of 1749; and of its continuance since, and spreading into Juliers, &c. We are not surprised to find that there is the same opposition to it that there was in Scotland, and in all other places where this blessed outpouring of the Holy Spirit was. The kingdom of Satan and his methods in supporting it, and of opposing the advancement of the Mediator's kingdom of grace, are much the same in all part of the earth. The spreading of lies, slanderous reports, and ridiculous stories of the subjects of this work, was one of the methods the evil spirit made use of to prejudice those at a distance against it, and to hinder its progress; and in this he had too great success. Yet this lasted but for a time, and the good work was rendered more illustrious and evident thereby: for many, both ministers and others, came from distant places to enquire into the nature of this work, and, by being eye-witnesses and conversing with the subjects of it, went away fully satisfied of its goodness, and of the falseness of the evil reports spread of it, blessed God for what they had seen; yea, some of those who came full of prejudice against it became the subjects of it: "They fell down on their faces, worshipped God, and reported that God was in such places of a truth."

About the beginning of this work in Scotland, many false reports were sent from New-England in anonymous pamphlets, letters, &c., from those in the opposition there, representing what had been of it in these provinces as enthusiasm and delusion; denying any remarkable work of conversion to be carried on; and magnifying imprudences, irregularities, and exceptionable things, which in some places were intermixed with this work, and which the most of the promoters and friends of it condemned as much as they, and opposed to the utmost of their power. But in a very little time, the falsehood of these reports were made manifest here, and occasioned more abundant, explicit, and public attestations to the goodness of this work in New-England, and the hopefulness of the subjects of it. It had also this good effect, that it made ministers called to be immediately concerned in this work here to watch diligently against the very first appearance of these exceptionable things, which, by the Divine blessing, had its desired effect: for, as may be observed from the above impartial Narrative, little if any of these things mixed with this work here. And it is to be hoped, that those worthy ministers of Christ in the Netherlands, whom the Lord of the vineyard may honour to be employed in this glorious work, will use the same caution.

We are informed that the same method of opposition is made use of in Holland against this blessed work, and that there are some who confidently report there, that this work in Scotland was all enthusiasm, that it is come to nothing, and that the subjects of it are fallen away, and become worse than they were before.

This hath occasioned a minister in Holland to renew his repeated entreaties to me, to finish my Narrative, by giving an account of what can be said of the perseverance of the hopeful subjects of this work. Others in this country have joined him in this desire. I have a letter from a gentleman of piety and good judgment, at some distance from this, who had seen a copy of the above minister's letter. He writes me as follows:— "He entreats you to publish something to show that the blessed work at Kilsyth, Cambuslang, &c., was not abortive; but that the happy fruits thereof endure. Dear sir, if I could say any thing further to the same purpose, gladly would I do it. You see in the above minister's letter, that even in that country this slander is propagated; that it is said all was fancy and enthusiastical fits, and the subjects of it fallen back to sin. Dear sir, doth not all this call you to do justice to the work of God; and not let it and the sincere followers of the Lamb be slandered and reproached?" There hath been no time since the beginning of this Narrative when the concluding of it with this Article could have been so seasonable as now, as has been already observed. I am therefore persuaded that by the wise and overruling providence of God, to whom all his works are known from the beginning; it hath been reserved to this time, when it serves to contradict those false and slanderous reports, and to promote the interests of religion, and the kingdom of

139

Jesus Christ in a church and country of all others most dear to us.

I shall therefore not only give a sincere and impartial account of what I know of the perseverance of the subjects of this work in this congregation and neighbourhood, but also insert the declarations of several well known ministers of the gospel in this church concerning the perseverance of many in their parishes, or otherwise known to them: some of which I have had by me for some time past, and others of them are newly received: and if there had been time for it many more might have been obtained and inserted here.

In the parish and congregation of Kilsyth, there were many awakened and under a work of conviction to public knowledge and observance, whose convictions and impressions ceased, without coming to any good issue, some sooner, some later. There have been some here under greater terrors and a sharper awakening than many of those were, who by grace appeared to attain a desirable and hopeful issue of their spiritual distress, who came to nothing — they rested short of Christ, became secure again, and returned to their former life. Some of these last were many weeks, if not months, under great terror and distress. Some of those who lost their impressions came to no saving issue, by being engaged too much in worldly affairs. "The cares of this life choked the word, and they became unfruitful." Some through ignorance, and not being diligent to learn the way of salvation through Jesus Christ; some through the influence of evil company, and consulting with flesh and blood; some through the outcry raised by the Seceders, that all their convictions were but delusions and from the Devil, one way or another they resisted the Holy Spirit, and provoked him to withdraw his influences, and so the work of the Spirit upon them ceased, and came to no saving issue.

There are instances of those under convictions, who not only returned to their former careless and sinful lives, but are worse than they were formerly, as they were expressly warned, from the word of God, would be the case, if their convictions issued not in their saving conversion. It hath happened unto them, as our blessed Lord declared to the Jews, "When the unclean spirit is gone out of a man, he walketh through dry places, seeking rest, and findeth none. Then he saith, I will return into my house from whence I came out; and when he is come, he findeth it empty, swept, and garnished. Then goeth he, and taketh with himself seven other more wicked than himself, and then enter in and dwell there; and the last state of that man is worse than the first." This hath befallen a few who were under notorious awakening and convictions; but a greater number who were under degrees of awakening and conviction, appearing only in the general reformation of the parish for a time. Of which general reformation there is a particular account given in the former part of this Narrative. This hath long since ceased, and the gross sins of drunkenness, uncleanness, profaning the holy name of God, strife and debate, abound among these more than ever I knew in this place, unless it was at the time of my first coming to it. It is true indeed that there are several both of the notoriously awakened, and of those whose impressions appeared in some outward reformation, who continue more reformed outwardly than they were before this work, upon whom I can discern no evidence of their having undergone a saving change. They seem to rest upon their convictions and amendment of life, as their righteousness in the sight of God; and to rest in them without seeking any thing further.

This was feared and looked for from the beginning of

this extraordinary work. We never either thought or said that such a work of awakening and conviction was saving conversion, though we looked upon it then, and continue still to judge it, the work of the Holy Spirit, answering many good ends to the glory of God, and the real good of this part of his church. Neither did I ever pronounce such persons converted because of their outcries and other effects of their inward fear, though they continued long in such a situation; or because of any steps or degrees they attained of mere conviction. Many miscarrying under a work of conviction is and always hath been as ordinary in the church as many blossoms perishing every year without coming to fruit, yea, many more than ever ripen. It is judged with great probability that there are few who live any long time under the preaching of the word but who are under some convincing work of the Holy Spirit some time in their life; and yet the far greater part live and die unconverted. This is the deplorable case of many more than what is generally imagined; and where the new creature is perfectly formed in one awakened person, there are many abortions and miscarriages.

Although there hath been so many awakened who sooner or later lost all their uneasy impressions without coming to rest in Christ; yet, blessed be the God and Father of our Lord Jesus Christ, there were a considerable number who gave good reason to me and others to hope well of them, and charitably to conclude that they had undergone a saving change. It is known to several of my brethren, that I was not forward in expressing my good thoughts of the attainments of particular persons, but rather upon the reserve and slow in what concerned this. But what could I do with those who, after often-repeated instruction, converse with them, and inquiry into the progress of this work upon them, gave such an

142

account of their convictions and their progress — of their being enlightened in the saving knowledge of Christ — of their receiving him by faith in all his offices — of their consolation and other exercies, as agreed with the Holy Scriptures, corresponded with the experiences of formerly converted persons, and was evidenced by the outward universal reformation of their lives? Was I not to look upon all this as good ground to conclude in charity that they were become real Christians? And might I not, when I found it was needful, declare to such persons, that such things, if they were in them as they declared, were those things that accompany salvation; and that though they were sometimes in darkness, yet they were now light in the Lord, and should be very careful to walk as children of the light; warning them in the strongest terms, of the dreadfulness of the sin and danger of backsliding and apostacy, with other suitable exhortations and directions? These, a very few excepted, continue to this day to have their conversation such as becometh the gospel, and to manifest their faith by good works, to the glory of God. Three or four of these excepted have fallen into gross sin, from which I hope they have recovered by repentance, and bring forth fruits meet for it.

There are two things I expressly assert, and am able to make good, that of those who were judged hopefully converted, and made a public profession of religion, there have been fewer instances of scandal and apostacy than might be and was expected: yea, further, that in proportion to their numbers there hath been fewer instances of apostacy of these than of those who gave me hopes of their conversion in former years.

It is most certain, that the great earnestness appearing in them by their extraordinary diligence in external duties, outward expressions of their affections, and their employing what many thought too much time in religious concerns, is ceased; and they are come to live and to mind the lawful affairs and business of this life as others before them did. The ceasing of this earnestness was one of the principal reasons why enemies concluded, and gave out, that all the good these persons pretended to, and were thought to have attained, was evanished and gone: whereas, if it had continued they would have objected that it could be no work of God that hindered such persons from being useful to themselves and others in the stations and relations wherein he had placed them. This hath also proven discouraging to some of these Christians themselves, and made them call in question the goodness of their state. But such would do well to remember that, as Mr. Henry expresseth it, "we cannot judge of ourselves by the pangs of affliction: these may be more vehement and sensible at first; and their being less so afterwards ought not to discourage us. The fire may not blaze so high as it did, and yet may burn hotter and stronger."

It is to be lamented, that many of them have lost much of the liveliness they had for some years, and are seized with that spiritual deadness which at this day is so much the sad disease of the people of God every where in this church. And I am afraid that the Lord hath the charge against us he had against the church at Ephesus, "Nevertheless, I have somewhat against thee, because thou hast left thy first love." Some of them are sensible and complain of it, and I hope are using proper means for help, though I am persuaded it is but faintly. They also appear at times to be under greater degrees of concern than others in hearing the word of God. There are also some who continue not only living but lively Christians. And yet the Lord's message to the foresaid church of Ephesus is undoubtedly to be applied to the most of his people here, both former and later converts, "Remember therefore from whence thou art fallen, and repent, and do the first works; or else I will come unto thee quickly, and remove thy candlestick out of its place, except thou repent."

It is no evidence that the hopeful subjects of the extraordinary work here do not persevere, that several of the numerous societies for prayer are ceased, more than it is that all the real Christians in this parish were fallen away because all these societies were ceased for some considerable time before this work appeared here. Some of these societies are failed, because the members of them, being single and unmarried persons, are removed to other places at a distance either by marriage, or entering into some other families as servants. In some cases two smaller societies are become one. And in some instances persons have forsaken these meetings, and particular meetings have ceased, without being able to assign any satisfying reason for it; and no other can be given besides degrees of backsliding and their love waxing cold. This last hath been the sad case of as many of those who were professors before this extraordinary work as of those who have become such since. If there be no more to bring into the account, it will neither infer apostacy, nor that such persons were never converted. Elder Christians, who either never joined in any society for prayer, or who have given up with them after joining, would think they were hardly dealt with to be censured as apostates, or persons who never had a saving work, merely upon this account; and is it not as hard and unjust to treat any of the hopeful subjects of the late good work after this sort? and yet both these denominations have great reason to charge themselves with shameful backsliding, and to be afraid lest, having begun to depart from the living God, it proceed from an evil heart of unbelief, and may at length issue in total and final apostasy. If he that standeth should take heed lest he fall, much more should he who in some instances and degrees hath fallen already, and is not what once he appeared to be.

I have this further to add concerning the hopeful subjects we speak of, that I never had such satisfaction and clearness in admitting any others to the Lord's table as I have had in admitting them; and that few or none besides gave me such comfort and satisfaction concerning their spiritual state and condition as these do when they are sick and dying or in any other state of trial and affliction. A few of them, after that they had lived several months or years, to outward appearance, worthy of the Lord, to all well-pleasing, have been taken from us by death. Those who made the greatest noise about forbearing to pronounce this extraordinary work good untill we should see the after-lives of the subjects of it, and whether they persevered or not in the goodness they professed, must acknowledge, if they deal fairly and candidly, that these persons were hopefully converted; seeing that they continued to walk like such, from the supposed time of their conversion unto the end of their trial for eternity. And is it not reasonable, and a part of that charity which "thinketh no evil, and hopeth all things," to hope that those who have continued so many years blameless and harmless, as the children of God without rebuke, in the midst of a perverse and crooked nation, among whom they shine as lights, shall continue so unto the end?

For this reason I required the following Attestations of the kirk session to the perseverance of those persons only who had been blameless in their lives, according to the measure of good Christians; leaving out those who had fallen into gross sins, although they had given good evidences of their repentance; as also those who had some things which some one or other of the session complained of, and wanted to have them admonished for, even where these things, if true, were not sufficient grounds to doubt of their conversion. Yea, it was said in the session by some of its members, and not contradicted by others, that there were several omitted in the list of persons proposed to the session as hopeful as those who were inserted, and who are from time to time admitted to the Lord's table; and who would have been admitted if the holy supper had been dispensed in the congregation at this time; though, indeed, after warnings and admonitions suitable to the verity and importance of the complaints made. But I choose rather to lessen the number of the persons attested, to cut off occasion of caviling and objection from those who desire and wait for it.

Chapter 9

Revival at Cambuslang

Sir, As the report of the good work at Cambuslang, which has for several weeks engaged the attention of numbers in this city and neighbourhood, is now spread over a great part of the nation, it is no wonder that one who lives at the distance you do should be curious to have a true relation of it; and as I would be glad of any opportunity to serve you, it is very agreeable to me to think I can gratify you in this matter; especially in what concerns the people in that parish and some others near to it, having had opportunity to converse fully with the minister of Cambuslang, and with many of the people there who are under this spiritual exercise, and also with some other ministers who have several in their parishes that appear to be under the same happy impressions.

There is one thing in the outset I must apprise you of, namely, that I am to confine myself to a simple narration of facts, as the evidences on which the opinion of many concerning the present happy change that is wrought on the people is founded; without entering into any reasoning, but leaving it to yourself to draw proper conclusions from the facts, after comparing them with scripture rules and instances.

I must also acquaint you, as it was natural to expect when, on a singular occasion of this sort, great numbers of people from adjacent towns and country came flocking to a place that became so remarkable, that in such a promiscuous multitude some counterfeits would readily happen, it was the early care of ministers who interested themselves most in that matter, to enter into a strict examination of those who appeared to be under a more than ordinary concern, so as to obtain satisfaction to themselves whether the work was solid, being justly apprehensive that the powers of darkness would not fail to employ their devices to bring contempt on what might tend so much to the honour of the gospel.

In those watchful endeavours it must be owned that some imposters were found to have mixed with the sincere; but there is reason to bless God that, so far as yet appears, they have been very few; and as these have been severely rebuked, so the most awful warnings have been given against all such insincere pretensions, which warnings, there is ground to believe, have had very good effects.

Now, sir, to give the short history of this matter.

The minister of that parish, in his ordinary course of sermons for nearly a twelve month before this work began, had been preaching on those subjects which tend most directly to explain the nature and prove the necessity of regeneration, according to the different lights in which that important matter is represented in Holy Scripture; and for some months before the late remarkable events, a more than ordinary concern about religion appeared among that people, one good evidence of which was, that about the end of January last a petition was given in to the minister, subscribed by about ninety heads of families, desiring a weekly lecture should be set up, which was readily granted, and the day fixed on was Thursday, as the most convenient for the temporal interests of the parish.

On Monday, the 15th of February, there was a general meeting at the minister's house of the particular societies for prayer, which had subsisted in the parish for several years before; on Tuesday there was another meeting for prayer there, the occasion of which was a concert with several serious Christians elsewhere about solemn prayer relating to the public interests of the gospel, in which concert only a small number of people in Cambuslang were engaged at first, but others getting notice of it desired to join, and were admitted. The people who met for prayer these two days apprehended that they had been so well employed and found so much leisure for it that they had a third meeting on Wednesday; but on all these three days they returned timeously in the evening to their own houses — so far is it from being true that they rushed from some of these meetings to the church and continued immured there for some days and nights, as was reported.

Before Thursday, February 18th, they had weekday sermons only on Thursdays, according to the above mentioned desire of the parish; and before that day, though several particular persons came to the minister from time to time under deep concern about their salvation, yet there came no great numbers together.

But on that day after sermon a considerable number of people, reckoned by some present about fifty, came together to the minister's house under convictions and alarming apprehensions about the state of their souls, and desiring to speak with him.

From this unexpected number coming in an evening, in so great distress, and the necessity of the minister's exhorting them in general, and conversing with many of them separately, you will easily perceive that he behoved to spend that night with them, as he did most part of two or three more since this work began, which is now about twelve weeks.

After this numbers daily resorted to that place, some to hear the word, some to converse with people who were under this remarkable concern, and others with different views; and the desires and exigencies of those were such that the minister found himself obliged, without any previous intimation, to provide them daily sermon, a few days excepted, and after sermon usually to spend some time with them in exhortations, prayers, and singing of psalms, being especially encouraged thereto by the extraordinary success with which God was pleased, from time to time, to bless his own ordinances, insomuch that, by the best information that could be had, the number of persons awakened to a deep concern about salvation, and against whom there are no known exceptions as yet, has amounted to above three hundred. And, through divine mercy, the work seems to be still making considerable progress every week, and more for some weeks of late than sometimes formerly.

Of the number just now mentioned the far greater part have given already, both to ministers and other serious Christians, a good account of what they have felt in their convictions and humiliation for sin, of the way of their relief by faith in the mercy of God through Christ, and of the change they feel in the prevalent inclinations and dispositions of their hearts.

As to their devotion and other parts of their practice, which is that which chiefly attracts the attention and regard of this country, there are comfortable accounts given of it by those who have the best and most frequent opportunities of knowing their daily behaviour.

The parish of Cambuslang being of so small extent that most of the people live within a mile of the church, and some who have the best intelligence being almost every day with the minister, he and they have abundant opportunities to know the practices of such of the people I am speaking of as live within their bounds, and the account they give of it is, that they appear to be in a very hopeful way; and the like good accounts of such of those people as belong to the neighbouring parishes are given by several ministers and others.

Among the particular good fruits already appearing, both in Cambuslang and elsewhere, the following instances seem very encouraging: a visible reformation of the lives of persons who were formerly notorious sinners; particularly, the laying aside of cursing and swearing and drinking to excess, among those who were addicted to these practices; remorse for acts of injustice, and for violation of relative duties, confessed to the persons wronged, joined with new endeavours after a conscientious discharge of such duties; restitution, which has more than once been distinctly and particularly inculcated in public since this work began; forgiving of injuries; all desirable evidences of fervent love to one another, to all men, and even to those who speak evil of them; and among those people both in Cambuslang and other parishes, more affectionate expressions of regard than ever to their own ministers, and to the ordinances dispensed by them; the keeping up divine worship in families where it was neglected very often by some and entirely by others; the erecting of new societies for prayer, both of old and young, partly within the parish, where no less than twelve such societies are newly begun, and partly elsewhere, among persons who have been awakened on this occasion; and together with all these things, ardent love to the Holy Scriptures, vehement thirsting after the public ordinances, earnest desires to get private instructions in their duty from ministers and others, with commendable docility and tractableness in receiving such instructions.

This thirst after knowledge is particularly remarkable in those who were most ignorant; several who cannot read, and some of them old persons, being so desirous to be better acquainted with the word of God that they are resolved to learn to read, and some of the younger sort actually putting themselves to school.

I would further add, that these good impressions have been made on persons of very different characters and ages; on some of the most abandoned as well as the more sober; on young as well as old: on the illiterate as well as the more knowing; on persons of a slower as well as those of a quicker and more sprightly genius; and, which seems to deserve special attention, on persons who were addicted to scoffing at sacred things, and at this work in particular at the beginning of it.

The sum of the facts I have represented to you is, that this work has been begun and carried on under the influence of the great and substantial doctrines of Christianity, pressing jointly, "the necessity of repentance towards God, of faith in the Lord Jesus Christ, and of holiness in all manner of conversation;" that it came after such preparatives as an extensive concern about religion gradually increasing; together with extraordinary fervent prayer in large meetings, particularly relating to the success of the gospel; that great and successful pains have been taken to discover and discountenance hypocritical pretences, and to warn people against what might have the least appearance of enthusiasm or delusion; that the account given by a very large number of people of their inward exercises and attainments seems to agree with the Scripture standard; and that they are bringing forth in practice "fruits meet for repentance," comprehending the several branches of piety, and of the most substantial morality that can entitle men to the regard of the friends of religion and virtue.

And now, sir, I have given you a plain and simple account of the most material facts relating to this extraordinary work at Cambuslang, and those awakened there belonging to other parishes, together with the proper documents by which these facts are supported; in all which I have avoided disputing, and studied brevity.

I leave it to you to judge how far such facts make it evident that this work is from God, when (to use the words of a pious divine treating of a subject of the same nature) "He that was formerly a drunkard lives a sober life, when a vain, light, and wanton person becomes grave and sedate, when the blasphemer becomes a praiser of God, when carnal joy is turned into heaviness, and that professedly on account of their souls' condition; when the ignorant are filled with knowledge of divine things, and the tongue that was dumb in the things of God speaks the language of Cannan, when secure sinners have been roused with a witness about the state of their souls, Luke, xi, 21, 22, those who were ignorant can speak skilfully about religious things, and even the graceless are increased in knowledge, swearers drop their oaths and speak reverently of God: vain persons who minded no religion, but frequented taverns and frolics, passing their time in filthiness, foolish talking and jesting, or singing paltry songs, do now frequent christian societies (for prayer), seek christian conversation and talk of soul-concerns, and choose to express their mirths in pslams and hymns and spiritual songs: they who were too sprightly to be devout, and esteemed it an unmanly thing to shed tears for their souls' state, have mourned as for an only son, and seemed to be in bitterness as for a first born,Zech. xii, 10: — And persons who came to mock at the lamentations of others have been convinced, and by free grace proselyted to

such ways as they formerly despised. I am, yours, &c.
May 8th, 1742.

Attestation to the facts in the preceding Narrative by Mr. M'Culloch, Minister at Cambuslang.

May 8th, 1742.

I have perused the preceding short Narrative, and can attest the facts contained in it; partly from personal knowledge, partly from the most credible informations; but think it a loss that it is not more full. I have seen a larger Paper compiled by different hands; which, besides the facts related in this, contains several useful reasonings, tending to prove that the favourable judgment formed by many, and even by some who through want of due information hesitated at first about this work, is supported by all that kind of evidence that things of this nature are capable of in such a space of time. And consequently, that there is good ground to hope that the Divine blessing, the confirmation arising from perseverance will be daily increasing, as hitherto it has been.

The said large Paper contained also a vindication of this work from various objections, and false and injurious aspersions thrown on it in print, by some who have not yet appeared to own their accusations; which in justice they ought to do or retract them. But though it has not been thought expedient to publish that larger Account at present, I understand the Compilers of it can easily, if it shall be thought needful afterwards, prepare it for the press.

For my own part, I desire to join in hearty prayers with the people of God, that he "may revive his work in the midst of the years," in this and all the churches, and make it to triumph over all opposition; and conclude with the words of the prophet, "Not by might nor by power, but by my Spirit, saith the Lord. Who art thou, O great mountain? before Zerubbabel [the Lord Jesus Christ] thou shalt become a plain, and he shall bring forth the head-stone thereof with shoutings, crying, Grace, grace unto it."

WILLIAM M'CULLOCH.

An Account of the Second Sacrament at Cambuslang: in a Letter from Mr. M'Culloch to a Brother.

Reverend and dear Brother, You know that we had the sacrament of the Lord's Supper dispensed here on the eleventh of July last. It was such a sweet and agreeable time to many, that a motion was made by Mr. Webster, and immediately seconded by Mr. Whitefield, that we should have another such occasion again in this place very soon. The motion was very agreeable to me, but I thought it needful to deliberate before coming to a resolution. The thing proposed was indeed extraordinary, but so had the work in this place been for several months past. Care was therefore taken to acquaint the several meetings for prayer with the motion, who relished it well, and prayed for direction to those concerned to determine in this matter. The Session met next Lord's day, and taking into consideration the divine command to celebrate this ordinance often, joined with the extraordinary work that had been here for some time past, and understanding that many who had met with much benefit to their souls at the last solemnity had expressed their earnest desire of seeing another in this place shortly, and hearing that there were many who intended to have joined at the last occasion, but were kept back through inward discouragements or outward obstructions, and were wishing soon to see another opportunity of that kind here, to which they might have access; it was therefore resolved (God willing) that the sacrament of the Lord's Supper should be again dispensed in this parish on the third Sabbath of August next, being the fifteenth day of that month. And there was first one day, and then another, at some distance of time from that, appointed for a general meeting at the manse of the several societies for prayer in the parish, who accordingly met there on the days appointed, with some other Christians from places in the neighbourhood: and when the manse sometimes could not conveniently hold them they went to the church; and at one of these meetings, when light failed them in the church, a good number, of their own free motion, came again to the manse, and continued at prayers and praises together till about one o'clock next morning.

The design of these meetings, and the business which they were accordingly employed in (besides singing of psalms and blessing the name of God together) was to ask mercy of the God of heaven to ourselves; to pray for the Seceders and others who unhappily oppose this work of God here and in some other parts where it takes place, that God would forgive their guilt in this matter, open their eyes, remove their prejudices, and convince them that it is indeed his work, and give them repentance to the acknowledgment of this truth; that the Lord would continue and increase the blessed work of conviction and conversion here and in other places where it is begun in a remarkable measure, and extend it to all the corners of the land; and that he would eminently countenance the dispensing of the sacrament of the Holy Supper a second time in this place, and thereby make the glory of this latter solemnity to exceed that of the former. Much of the Lord's gracious presence was enjoyed at these meetings for prayer, returns of mercy were vouchsafed in part, and are still further expected and hoped for.

This second sacramental occasion did indeed much excel the former, not only in the number of ministers, people, and communicants, but, which is the main thing, in a much greater measure of the power and special presence of God in the observation and sensible experience of multitudes that were attending.

The ministers that assisted at this solemnity were Mr. Whitefield, Mr. Webster from Edinburgh, Mr. Maclaurin and Mr. Gillies from Glasgow, Mr. Robe from Kilsyth, Mr. Currie from Kinglassie, Mr. M'Kneight from Irvine, Mr. Bonner from Torphichen, Mr. Hamilton from Douglas, Mr. Henderson from Blantyre, Mr. Maxwell from Rutherglen, and Mr. Adam from Cathcart. All of them appeared to be very much assisted in their work. Four of them preached on the Fast day, four on Saturday, on Sabbath I cannot well tell how many, and five on Monday; on which last day it was computed that above twenty-four ministers and preachers were present. Old Mr. Bonner, though so frail that he took three days to ride eighteen miles, from Torphichen to Cambuslang, yet his heart was so set upon coming here that he could by no means stay away, and when he was helped up to the tent, preached three times with great life, and returned with much satisfaction and joy. Mr. Whitefield's sermons on Saturday, Sabbath, and Monday, were attended with much power, particularly on Sabbath night about ten, and that on Monday, several crying out, and a very great but decent weeping and mourning was observable through the auditory. On Sabbath evening while he was serving some tables, he appeared to be so filled with the love of God as to be in a kind of extacy or transport, and communicated with much of that blessed frame. Time would fail me to speak of the evidences of the power of God coming along with the rest of the assistants; and I am in part prevented by what is noticed by Mr. Robe in his Narrative.

The number of people that were there on Saturday and Monday was very considerable. But the number present at the three tents on the Lord's day was so great that, so far as I can hear, none ever saw the like since the Revolution in Scotland, or even any where else, at any sacramental occasion: some have called them fifty thousand; some forty thousand; the lowest estimate I hear of, with which Mr. Whitefield agrees, who has been much used to great multitudes, and forming a judgment of their number, makes them to have been upwards of thirty thousand.

The number of communicants appears to have been about three thousand. The tables were double, and the double table was reckoned to contain one hundred and fourteen, or one hundred and sixteen, or one hundred and twenty communicants. The number of tables I reckoned had been but twenty-four: but I have been since informed that a man who sat near the tables and kept a pen in his hand, and carefully marked each service with his pen, assured that there were twenty-five double tables or services, the last table wanting only five or six persons to fill it up. And this account seems indeed the most probable, as agreeing nearly with the number of tokens distributed, which was about three thousand. And some worthy of credit, and that had proper opportunities to know, gave it as their opinion, that there was such a blessed frame fell upon the people, that if there had been access to get tokens, there would have been a thousand more communicants than what were.

This vast concourse of people, you may easily imagine, came not only from the city of Glasgow, and other places near by, but from many places at a considerable distance: it was reckoned there were two hundred communicants from Edinburgh, two hundred from

Kilmarnock, one hundred from Irvine, and one hundred from Stewarton. It was observed, that there were some from England and Ireland here at this occasion: a considerable number of Quakers were hearers: a great many of those that had formerly been Seceders were hearing the word, and several of them were communicants. A youth that has a near view to the ministry, and had been for some time under great temptations that God's presence was no more to be enjoyed either in the church or among the Seceders, communicated here, and returned with great joy, full of the love of God.

There was a great deal of outward decency and regularity observable about the tables. Public worship began on the Lord's day just at half past eight in the morning. My action sermon, I think, was reasonably short: the third or fourth table was being served at twelve o'clock, and the last table about sunset; when that was done, the work was closed with a few words of exhortation, prayer, and praise, the precentor having so much daylight as to let him see to read four lines of a psalm. The passes to and from the tables were with great care kept clear for the communicants to come and go. The tables filled so quickly, that often there was no more time between one table and another than to sing four lines of a psalm. The tables were all served in the open air, beside the tent, below the brae; the day was temperate — no wind or rain in the least to disturb. Several persons of considerable rank and distinction who were elders most cheerfully assisted our elders in serving the tables, such as the Honourable Mr. Charles Erskine, Advocate, Bruce of Kennet, Esq., Gillen of Wallhouse, Esq., Mr. Warner of Ardeer, and Mr. Wardrope, Surgeon in Edinburgh.

But what was most remarkable was the spiritual glory of this solemnity, I mean the gracious and sensible presence of God. Not a few were awakened to a sense of sin, and their lost and perishing condition without a Saviour. Others had their bands loosed, and were brought into the marvelous liberty of the sons of God. Many of God's dear children have declared, that it was a happy time to their souls, wherein they were abundantly satisfied with the goodness of God in his ordinances, and filled with all joy and peace in believing. I have seen a letter from Edinburgh, the writer of which says, that "having talked with many Christians in that city who had been here at this sacrament, they all owned, that God had dealt bountifully with their souls at this occasion." Some that attended here declared, that they would not for a world have been absent from this solemnity. Others cried, Now let thy servants depart in peace, from this place, since our eyes have seen thy salvation here. Others wished, if it were the will of God, to die where they were attending God in his ordinances, without ever returning again to the world or their friends, that they might be with Christ in heaven, as that which is incomparably best of all.

I thought it my duty to offer these few hints concerning this solemnity, and to record the memory of God's great goodness to many souls at that occasion. And now I suppose you will by this time find yourself disposed to sing the ninety-eighth Psalm at the beginning, or the close of the seventy-second, or some other Psalm of praise. May our exalted Redeemer still go on from conquering to conquer, untill the whole earth be filled with his glory. Amen, so let it be. In him, I am, Yours, &c.

WILLIAM M'CULLOCH.

Attestation, of the Rev. Mr. M'Culloch, Minister of Cambuslang, relating to the Fruits and Effects of the

Extraordinary Work at that Place, in 1742, in a Letter to the Rev. Mr. Robe.

Cambuslang Manse, April 30, 1757.

Rev. and dear Brother, Hearing that you are very soon, as a close to your Narrative, to publish some Attestations to the fruits of the revival of religion in this country in the year 1742, at the desire of some ministers I drew up and herewith send you my Attestation relating to the effects of the extraordinary work here in 1742, which you may publish along with your own Attestation and those of others. When the God of all grace is pleased, in infinite mercy, to send a revival of religion to a church or any particular corner in it, among other artifices whereby Satan and his instruments endeavour to obstruct its progress, a very usual and successful one is to raise prejudices against it in people's minds, by suggesting and alleging, that though the like awakenings and promising appearances, (or as opposers use to speak, religious stirs and commotions) formerly obtained in as high or even higher degree elsewhere, yet there was no good followed, but a great deal of evil.

Thus, as I am credibly informed, it is at the time of the present revival of religion, in several places of the United Provinces, as particularly, at Nieukirk, Rheid, Aalten, Groningen, &c., while the friends of that work there take notice how much it resembles the work at Cambuslang in 1742, the opposers readily grant there is a resemblance; but then they add, that the work at Cambuslang in 1742 never produced any valuable effect, that the subjects of that work are worse than before, that it was schismatical work, &c.

In order therefore to set this matter in a clear light, and that I might be able to give a brief but just account of a work that happened in a parish whereof I have the pastoral inspection and charge, and which I cannot but look upon to have been a glorious work of God's grace, I thought it my duty to make a particular inquiry concerning the behaviour of the known subjects of the work at Cambuslang in 1742, that is, those persons not only living in the parish of Cambuslang, but who came from many other places, near or more remote, and who upon restoring to Cambuslang, in 1742, are known to have there fallen under awakenings, convictions, and a deep concern about eternal salvation, for the first time, or at least, the first time that their convictions and concern seemed to prove effectual, and to come to a gracious issue.

I do not here propose to speak (if it be not a few words by the by) of those who resorted hither in 1742, and who were true Christians before that. Of these there were many hundreds, I doubt not but I may say thousands, from places near and far off, who then flocked hither, and joined in hearing of the word and great numbers of them, upon producing sufficient testimonials, were admitted to partake of the sacrament of the Lord's Supper; and thereby the number of communicants, which here used to be but about four or five hundred before 1742, came to be greatly increased in that and following years; so that at the second sacrament the number of communicants in 1742 was reckoned at three thousand; in 1743, about two thousand; in 1744, about fifteen hundred; in 1745, about thirteen hundred; in 1746, about twelve hundred, &c., and all along to this present year 1751, the number of communicants here has greatly exceeded what used to be before 1742.

The unweariedness of the Lord's people in religious exercises at these times, especially at the sacramental occasion in 1742, 1743, and 1744, was wonderful. What eager attention to hearing the word as upon the stretch and for eternity! What an awful, serious, solemn air appeared in the manner of their worship! What vehement workings of joy and sorrow and other passions appearing in their looks! What engaged attendance on God in his ordinances! hearing three sermons on each of these three days, Thursday and Saturday and Monday; double the number on the communion Sabbath, besides partaking of the sacrament, joining in public prayers and praises, spending almost the whole of Saturday and Sabbath nights in praises and prayers with others or apart by themselves.

And their attainments were answerable to their exercises: thus at least it was with many of them, according to the account they gave to me, or to others, from whom I had it, and whom I could entirely credit. Many attained to the full assurance of faith, had a sense of God's love top them, and the exercise of ardent love to him, and after believing in Christ, were sealed with the Holy Spirit of promise. Some eminently pious ministers, who assisted here, testified, that they had never seen so much of heaven on earth. A very aged and worthy minister at going away from this, cried out at the stair-head in the manse, "Now, Lord, lettest thou thy servant depart in peace, for mine eyes have seen thy salvation:" others of them after going home, wrote, that they would not for a world have been absent from Cambuslang, or missed what of God they enjoyed there.

But passing from speaking further of those who were true Christians before their coming here in 1742, I proceed to speak a little of those hearers who in the parable of the sower and the seed are compared to the highway-side ground, the stony ground, and the thorny ground, and then of those made good ground, where the word took root and prospered.

I. There were those who may be compared to the highway-side ground, who hear the word, and understand it not, through their own fault; because they take no heed to the word and take no hold of it, nor come with any design to get good, but commonly for fashion's sake, to see and to be seen, and mind not what is said; so that what comes in at the one ear goes out at the other, and makes no impression; and the Devil, that wicked one, comes and catcheth away that which was sown, and makes an easy prey of such careless trifling hearers. And such, no doubt, made a part of the vast multitudes that assembled here in 1742, though it must be owned that there was generally a more close engaged attention to the word, by what one could judge from outward appearance, than what is ordinary.

II. There were a sort of hearers of the word here in 1742 who might be called the stony-ground hearers, who were much affected with the word while they were hearing it, or for a short time, and yet received no saving benefit by it. The motions of soul they had answerable to what they heard were but a mere flash, like Ezekiel's hearers to whom he was a lovely song, and Isaiah's hearers that seemed to delight to know God's ways, or Herod who heard John Baptist gladly, and others who rejoiced in his lights; and yet all these came to no good issue. And thus many here in 1742 received the word with gladness, and yet came to nothing — by and by they were offended.

III. There were some here in 1742 who were much affected in hearing the word and other acts of worship, and appeared to be such as in the parable are called the thorny-ground hearers; these held out longer than the stony-ground hearers, and yet at length cam to no better issue than they. These seemed for a good while to have a mighty concern about religious matters, but having never been born again by the incorruptible seed of the word — the great commanding overswaying principle of

165

the love of God above all other objects having never been put into their souls, and the heart having never been crucified to the world by a virtue and power flowing into it from the death and cross of Christ eyed by faith — the thorns of worldly cares and lusts, murmuring and unthankfulness, and inordinate fancies of what they would be in the world, came at length to sink them gradually into worldliness and sensuality; and after they had for a time escaped the pollutions of the world, through the knowledge of the Lord and Saviour Jesus Christ, they appear now to be entangled therein and overcome, and the latter end is like to be worse with them than the beginning.

It must be owned that there is considerable number (though what number I cannot determined) of these three several sorts of hearers already mentioned that have greatly backslidden since 1742, and are still going on in their defection and apostacy, and enlarging the breach between God and them, and do not seem to be once thinking or resolving on a penitent return to God and their duty: but, blessed be his name, there are some few of these (though alas! but a very few, from what I know) who seem to be greatly humbled for their revoltings in heart, and outbreakings in life, and whose souls are echoing back to the Lord's call to backsliders to return, saying, "Behold, we come unto thee, for thou art the Lord our God."

Before I proceed to speak of the fourth sort of hearers, compared to the good ground, I would offer a few remarks as to the three sorts already described, from one or other of which the backsliders came, and how they came to be so.

(1.) As to the first sort, compared to the highwayside-ground hearers, these may be divided into three classes, 1. There was no doubt a considerable number of thoughtless careless persons, who came here for fashion's sake, without any care to have their hearts prepared for receiving the seed of the word, or attending to it seriously when they came, or to have that seed covered by after-meditation and prayer: and as to these, it could not be expected that they should continue in that good which they never had, though they have fallen from that good they once seemed to have. 2. There were some that were gross counterfeits, who, a little after the awakening broke out here in 1742, crowded in among the really distressed, and observing and imitating their manner, pretended to be also in spiritual distress, when they were no such thing. But these were detected to be mere pretenders, either by their own confession soon after, or were plainly enough discerned to be so by others: and these being early discovered and checked (especially with the assistance of ——— ——— at Glasgow,) the number of these counterfeits, from what I know, was never any way considerable, and in a short time they disappeared, from what we could observe or hear. There were also numbers of idle boys in Glasgow, apprentices and others, who pretending or seeming to be under some concern about their souls, came often out to Cambuslang, to hear and join in prayer in the fields together, as they pretended: but these appearances with them generally came to nothing, and they brought much reproach on the work here, by so often leaving their masters' work, and strolling idly through the fields. 3. There were those who came here in 1742 with a design to find matter of diversion, or to cavil, and to mock such as were in spiritual distress. The bands of such mockers were no doubt generally made stronger by their so coming, and so behaving when they came: and yet some of these were made happy monuments of victorious grace and of sovereign preventing mercy themselves: A remarkable instance of which I had lately sent me in a letter, from an aged and experienced Christian of great integrity, whom I can fully credit, especially in testifying what he cannot but certainly know. Part of which letter I shall here subjoin; which I do the rather because it serves to confute what some opposers have asserted, that there are no instances of any gross vicious sinners reformed or converted at Cambuslang in 1742. Glory to God, there is a number of other instances of this sort that can be given.

"I have to say, for my own part," says the writer of said letter, "that I am able to go to death with it, that the Spirit of God was so powerfully at work in Cambuslang, that not only sinners who knew nothing of God before were reached both by conviction and conversion, but even saints themselves were made to attain to that which they had been strangers to in the matters of religion. I am able, if time would allow, to give a most satisfying account of now a few, both men and women, who I hope will bless God to all eternity for that happy time: particularly there were among others two young men, living not far from me, who came over to you, in 1742, on purpose to mock the work: and as they had formerly been horrid cursers and swearers, the one swore to the other, he would go to see the falling at Cambuslang, asking his comrade if he would go with him to that place. The other swore he would go too, but that they should not make him fall, for that he would run for it. And upon their going there together, they were both caught the same day, and for a quarter of a year after the continued under very deep convictions, and have ever since kept fellowship meetings weekly: and I have been sometimes with them, and heard them both pray and converse in Christian experience, to my great satisfaction."

As to the contents of this letter, I only add, 1. That the

writer of it, a little after writing it, sent me a very particular satisfying account of a considerable number of the subjects of the work here in 1742, known to him and living near him, as to their blameless walk from that time to this; 2. And as to these two youths, it is well known here, that instead of being able to run away, if either found himself in hazard of being affected, as they proposed, they fell both under awakenings together, or very nearly so, and were glad to get into a stable hard by, and to get to their prayers there, on their knees, among the horses; and 3. As to what these youths called the falling at Cambuslang, it was a way of speaking among mockers at that time, occasioned by their seeing some fall down in time of sermon.

As to the second and third sort, compared to the stony- and thorny-ground hearers, the greater number of those that afterwards proved remarkable backsliders were no doubt of this sort of hearers; and the greatest number of those that made the greatest noise were also of the same.

But more particularly, I remark here,

1. There were here in 1742 many instances of persons who in time of sermon fell under various bodily agitations and commotions, as crying out aloud, tremblings, faintings, or swoonings, falling down as dead, &c.; concerning which bodily seizures, I think we may safely affirm, that one cannot certainly conclude merely from these seizures, that he himself or another is under the influences of the Holy Spirit, either in convincing, comforting, or sanctifying the soul; because it is possible these seizures may proceed from the mere power of imagination, or some sudden fright or bodily disorder: nor yet should one suspect himself or another to be a stranger to the convincing, comforting, or sanctifying influences of the Holy Spirit, merely because of his being

unacquainted with these bodily seizures; because some are brought under a sense of a lost and perishing condition by nature, and by actual transgressions, with fewer terrors and less violence and distress than others; and are happily brought home to Christ in a more mild, gradual, and gentle manner — are allured by the displays of the love and loveliness of Christ, and sweetly drawn to him with cords of love and bands of a man.

2. Such is the strict and near union of soul and body, that when any thing much affects the one, the other is consequently affected also in proportion. Thus it is in many outward occurrences in life: when a remarkably sorrowful or joyful event is suddenly made known to persons equally concerned in it (as the sudden news brought to a family, that a beloved son of that family, abroad, is dead, or suppose tidings brought afterwards that he is alive, father and mother, brothers and sisters,) all would be affected, but they would be differently affected, and would show themselves outwardly to be so, according to their different tempers of mind and constitutions of body. And why may it not be rationally expected, that the unspeakably more awful and concerning tidings brought to men's ears in hearing of the word should deeply affect their minds; and that these inward affections should discover themselves outwardly also, according to persons' different tempers and constitutions; especially while the threatenings of the law and promises of the gospel are powerfully applied to particular hearers, by the Holy Spirit, as certainly and undeniably belonging to them?

3. By all that I can observe or hear, there are more of those that were under deep concern here in 1742, that appear still to persevere in a good way and in the gospel-becoming practice, that never cried out aloud in time of public worship, or that were never observably under

those bodily agitations above mentioned, than of those that were under such outward commotions, and that made the greatest noise. There are indeed some of both sorts whose exercises seem to have come to a gracious issue, but many more of the former than of the latter sort.

4. Some under a kindly sense of sin, as a dishonour done to an infinitely holy and glorious God, others under the terrors of the Lord that fell upon their consciences, and fear of perishing for ever, trembled and swooned and fell down as dead, or cried out aloud; but where there were only terrors and fears of wrath, and no kindly sense of the evil of sin, when these terrors came to abate and wear off, persons returned to their former sins and carnal security, and their awakenings left them as bad as they were before: by their quenching the Spirit, and shaking off their convictions, without improving them to seek after and apply to Christ the remedy, they contracted and fell under a greater degree of hardness and blindness than formerly.

5. There were also several here in 1742, who after they had been for some short time under much distress and terror, in fears of wrath, while hearing sermons or in other duties, have been all at once filled with transporting joys, and some of them have cried out aloud in the congregation, in some short expression of their joys: and upon inquiry afterward into the ground of these joys, it appeared that in some they took rise from a display or manifestation inwardly to the soul, in a heart-overcoming way, answerable to the outward displays of the glory of Christ in the gospel, or of his love or the fruits of it, or the person's interest in these, made evident; and these so far as I know still persevere; but in others these joys appeared to proceed from the person's hearing or reading some promise of Scripture, and strongly

apprehending that it belonged to them; whereupon they seemed to be filled all at once with transporting joys; and these have, many of them at least, fallen away; and from several instances of this kind we have known here we cannot but conclude, that great and strong terrors, by themselves, or when followed with sudden and extatic joys, are no certain arguments of a gracious change, nor of a person's being under saving influence.

6. When the heart has not been humbled and broken for sin and from it, and when the soul has not been first united to the Lord Jesus, and made one spirit with him, who is the fountain of life, where the person has not first accepted of Christ in his gracious gospel-offers, and closed with him in all his redeeming offices — outgates from distressing terrors, by sudden transporting joys, though appearing to be conveyed by means of some Scripture-promises, are always suspicious and delusory, and at best but the joy of the stony-ground hearers, who receive the word with joy and anon are offended. And of this sort we had several instances in 1742, some of them also appearing under a blooming profession in 1743, reckoning that the bitterness of eternal death and all danger of it was past; but the dominion of pride, worldliness, and other corruptions remaining unbroken in them, and finding the difficulties and disagreeableness to their unrenewed nature of a holy, humble, self-denying life, they were offended and displeased with that kind of life, and so fell away to former sensuality.

7. As to outcries in the time of public worship, it is best to avoid extremes. On the one hand, hearers would not indulge themselves in outcries in public when they are under no necessity to cry by overpowering fears or joys, and when they could refrain from crying if they were willing; for by crying in that case, they do in a culpable and disorderly manner mar the attention of others and

their own to the word of God's grace; and ministers would not set themselves industriously to excite such outcries among the hearers, but rather to set the terrors of the law, and the unsearchable riches of Christ, and the grace of the gospel before them, leaving it to God to take his own way with them, who can, if he pleased, order the outcries of some to the awakening of others; of which there have been some instances here. On the other hand, such hearers as can attend with calmness and composure would not too harshly censure those as mad and outrageous who at any time are necessitated to cry out in the congregation by overbearing joys or fears; nor would ministers too severely rebuke or charge every such person to hold their peace; because, though there may be hypocritical cries, yet the real griefs or joys of some serious or gracious souls may be such as they cannot contain them; and while they endeavour to stifle and give no vent to them, nature may receive a dangerous shock. Some such hearers in this place in 1742, endeavouring with all their might to restrain themselves from crying, fell ableeding at mouth or nose, or both, and continued to do so for a considerable time before the bleeding could be got stopt — to the great weakening of the person's own strength, and to the disturbing of others about them, a reat deal more than by the outcries of others.

8. Meantime we see the mine the Devil has been springing, for undermining true religion and serious godliness, and blowing up into the air the honour due to it. How deep his plot — how cunning his stratagems for that purpose! When he saw there was a number here under deep convictions, and a kindly concern about their salvation that was like to issue well, about the end of 1741 and beginning of 1742, in order to bring disgrace on that work of the Spirit of God, he quickly pitches on

several poor abandoned wretches, his salves of whom he had got fast hold and was not like to lose, and teaches some of them to mimic such as were in soul-distress, causes others of them to cry out publicly, and to fall down as dead for some time, representing to their fancies various objects in the air, when they were awake or asleep, and suggesting various things to their minds at the same time, urging them afterwards to tell what they saw or heard, as visions, dreams, or revelations from heaven, exciting them to go and join in meetings for prayer, and to hold on in this way under a high profession, some for weeks, some for months, and others for years; and then at length to push them into uncleanness, drunkenness, lying, cheating, and all abominations, even to the throwing off (with some) the very profession of religion; which it is to be wished they had never put on. Could a more dangerous mine be sprung, could a more effectual way be taken to make men turn Atheists and Deists, and to despise serious godliness, and all appearances of it, as if all had been mere sham, grimace, and pretence? And thus it was like to have been, had not God preserved a remnant of those that were then under awakenings, and enabled them, by the holiness of their after-lives, to give evidence of the gracious change then wrought on their hearts. And this leads to speak,

IV. Of the fourth sort in the parable, compared to the good ground hearers. I do not here speak of those who were as good ground before 1742, but of those whose hearts were then made good: who in hearing the word were then made to receive it so as in their after-life to bring forth the fruits of righteousness, though in different degrees, in some thirty-, in some sixty-, in others a hundred-fold. A temper of mind and course of life agreeable to the gospel, this is fruit that will abound to the account of those with whom it is found. And, glory to

God, setting aside all those that appeared under awakenings here in 1742, who have since remarkably backslidden, whether persisting in their backsliding, or returning from it, there is a considerable number of the then awakened that appear to bring forth such fruits. I do not talk of them at random, nor speak of their number in a loose, general, and confused way; but have now before me, at the writing of this, April 27th, 1751, a list of about four hundred persons awakened here at Cambuslang in 1742, who from that time to the time of their death, or to this, that is, for these nine years past, have been all enabled to behave in a good measure as becometh the gospel, by any thing I could ever see, and by the best information I could get concerning them by word or writing, from others of established characters for religion, who knew them and their manner of life all along.

But that what I say in this matter may not be misunderstood, I remark,

First, Negatively, 1. I do not hereby pretend to say, that they are free of all faults and follies, as if nothing at all amiss could be justly charged on any of them; but would only say, that after much inquiry made, from what I know, they have been helped, since the time of their awakening to their death, or to this time, to carry in a good measure, suitable to their Christian profession, proper charitable allowances and abatements being made for involuntary infirmities and imprudencies, common to them with other Christians in this imperfect state; and that they have not been suffered to fall into anything gross or openly offensive in their life.

2. I do not pretend to say that this list before me is complete, or contains the whole number of those awakened here in 1742 that persevere. It is to be hoped that many of those quite unknown to me may be as good

Christians as any of those that are in it. It is but very lately that I got particular accounts of a considerable number of them who are choice practical Christians of whom I knew nothing before. Opposers at no great distance, hearing of the falls and miscarriages of some of the awakened, immediately raised a great clamour and noise, as if all were come to nothing; and that noise, it seems, has reached Holland and other distant places: but there is ground to suspect, that the more narrow the inquiries into this work and what the effects of it are, it will still appear in a more favourable and advantageous light.

3. It is not meant that all the regularly behaving subjects of that work are yet alive to answer for themselves. It may be hoped in charity that many of them are gone to heaven: but those only of the now deceased subjects of this work are reckoned in this number who, from the time of their awakening here in 1742 to the time of their deaths, were enabled to persevere in the ways of God, without falling openly into anything offensive or unsuitable to their Christian profession. And these are the most unexceptionable of all others, as having by an edifying life given evidence of the gracious change wrought on their hearts, and then finished their course; and several, though not all of them, having finished it with joy, and died triumphantly, and in the full assurance of eternal life.

4. When I mention the work here in 1742, and such comfortable abiding effects of it; I would not have that work as producing any of those blessed effects ascribed to any creature, but that the entire glory of it should be given to God whose work it was. It is true that there were many ministers then came here, from places near and more remote, and some of them men of great eminence, who preached here at my desire, and I used also to

preach along with them at their desire; and several of these ministers, after public worship was over, also joined with me in exhortations to souls appearing in spiritual distress, who resorted to the manse. But what could all these avail without the Divine power and blessing? whoever plant or water, it is God that gives the increase: ministers are but instruments in his hand: no praise was due to the rams' horns, though Jericho's walls fell down at their blast. If God will vouchsafe that his Spirit shall breathe through ministers, or by his word in the mouth, it is God and not the means must have the praise. It is very fit and reasonable, that he who builds the temple should bear the glory: and Christ is both the foundation and founder of the church, and of every particular living temple in it, and even all in all: and therefore let all the glory be ascribed to him.

5. When I speak of so many persevering subjects of the work here in 1742, I do not pretend to determine that all these are converted. A true believer may, without extra-ordinary revelation, be infallibly assured, that he himself is in a state of grace, and shall persevere therein to salvation; and yet this is not the attainment of every true believer, nor perhaps of the greater part of believers: but the like assurance is not to be expected, in an ordinary way, with respect to the goodness of the state of others; "the white stone and new name" is known absolutely to none but those that receive it: the gift of discerning spirits, so as to have an absolute infallible knowledge of the goodness of another's state, is quite miraculous; and whatever of this gift obtained in the apostolic and primitive times, for any man now to pretend to it seems to be an assuming of what belongs to God alone; and to run into this plan in church-matters is to turn all into the wildest disorder and confusion. But,

Secondly, and Positively: Whatever justly determines

us to entertain favourable sentiments of others' being true Christians, and in a gracious state, will be found to agree to those persons I speak of; though no doubt, with a diversity, as among an equal number of other Christians. The holiness of some Christians shines so clearly in their lives as suffices to fund a moral certainty, or very high degree of probability, and even to exclude all reasonable ground of doubt concerning the goodness of their state; while other afford ground but for a lower degree of probability, yet enough on which to found a judgment of charity that they are in a gracious state; some of both these sorts are, no doubt, to be found among the persons of whom I now speak.

Now there are these two things especially upon which we found our charitable thoughts of others as true Christians, namely, a christian profession, joined with an answerable conversation, leaving the certain and final judging of hearts and states to God, who only can judge them with infallible certainty, we are bound in charity to think men are good men as long as their profession of faith and lives are agreeable to th word of God, the only rule of faith and life.

Some indeed further require, that persons who would have a place in their charity should give some account of their experiences of the grace of God: and this is what a great number, perhaps above a fourth part of the persevering subjects here in 1742, have done: they gave me very particular accounts of God's dealings with their souls, in their first awakenings and outgates, with their following soul-exercises and experiences, distresses, deliverances, and comforts , in 1742, 1743, and 1744, and some of them also continued these accounts to 1748. And I set down very many of these from their mouths, always in their own sense, and very much also in their own words: and many of these accounts have appeared to competent judges, to whom they have been shown and who have perused them with care, to be very rational and scriptural, and worthy to see the light; which perhaps may be done hereafter.

But passing these things at the time, and confirming ourselves to the two things before mentioned that usually and justly determined us to look upon others as Christians where they meet together a Christian profession with an answerable practice: and both concur here.

All the persevering subjects of the work here in 1742 agree in professing their faith in Christ the Mediator, by whose mediation alone we can come to God the Father as our God and Father in him, through the power and grace of the Holy Spirit: they all profess to hope for salvation according to the gospel plan, by the imputed righteousness of Christ, entitling to eternal life and all blessings; and the sanctifying influences of the Spirit of Christ, disposing for eternal life, and all holy services and enjoyments here and hereafter.

But then, as our Saviour allows us to judge of the tree by its fruits, and true faith must be showed by good works, or holy obedience in the life, these things are also manifest in the lives of the persevering subjects I speak of: I am not at present free to publish any of their names, or those of the attestors, nor is it at all proper or needful to do so; but all the above number are severally attested, either by ministers, elders, or private Christians of established character, who have known them and their manner of life from 1742, and all these Attestations in sum bear not only, that such persons they mention were awakened at Cambuslang in 1742, or were under convictions and remarkable concern there at that time, but that they have all along from that to their death, or to this time, behaved well, and as became their christian profession, charitable allowances, being made for

179

involuntary weaknesses and infirmities, as to other Christians, in this imperfect state, as is said before.

But beside these generals, I shall here subjoin a few particulars, partly from my own knowledge and observation, partly by credible information from others, relating to their temper and practice.

By the practice of justice and charity, relative duties, public-spiritedness, humility, meekness, patience, and a close and diligent attendance on gospel ordinances, heavenly-mindedness, watchfulness, against all sin, especially those sins that used formerly easily to beset them, &c., they adorn the doctrine of God our Saviour, glorify their heavenly Father, and excite others to do so on their account.

Those of them that were cursers and swearers have laid aside that language of hell, and have learned much of the language of heaven, and to speak with holy awe of God and things divine.

Such of them as used to be often out in taverns, drinking and playing at cards, &c., till very late, or morning-hours rather, for these nine years past, shun all occasions of that kind, and keep at home at night, spending the night in christian conference, things profitable for their families, and in secret and family-devotion. The formerly drunken or tippling sot, that used to lie in bed till eight or nine in the morning, till he slept out last night's drunkenness, for these nine years, gets up at three or four in the morning, and continues at reading his Bible and other books, secret prayer and meditation, &c., till seven or eight o'clock in the morning, that he calls his household together for family-devotion; and does the like in the evening and at night.

Some wives who before 1742 were at variance with their husbands, have since that time got on the ornament of a meek and quiet spirit, and live in much love and peace with them. Others, when the husband's passions break out against them in boisterous and stormy language, run to another room to their knees, asking of God forgiveness and a better temper to the husband, and patience and meekness to herself, and after some time, returns from her knees, with the law of kindness on her lips to the husband, telling him, he is the best husband she could have got; for that he is the occasion of her going oftener to her knees than probably she would have gone if she had got one more loving and kind.

The formerly covetous and worldly-minded and selfish have got a public spirit, and zealous concern for promoting the kingdom and glory of Christ in the conversion and salvation of souls; and for this end, are careful not only to live inoffensively themselves, but usefully to others, so as all about them may be the better for them: they join cheerfully to their ability, and some even beyond it, (so that I have sometimes seen it needful to check some of them for too large quotas or offers) in collections for promoting the interest of religion, or for the relief of those straits, in places near hand or far off: they carefully observe the times fixed in the concert for prayer, and joining at such times in earnest pleadings at a throne of grace, for the spreading and success of the gospel, and the outpourings of the Spirit from on high on the churches.

They flock with great eagerness to the hearing of the word, in the several places where they reside, and, "as new-born babes, desire the sincere milk of the word, that they may grow thereby." Such earnest desires, of a number in this parish, after the word encouraged me in the beginning of the year 1742 to set up a weekly lecture on Thursdays, and to continue it from that time to this, all the year round, and even in harvest too, only altering the time of it then to the evening, to which the reapers come running from the fields, where they had been toiling all day. At other times of the year, some servants of their own free motion and choice are known sometimes to have sit up all night at their master's work, that they might have liberty to attend the weekly lecture next day without giving their master cause to complain.

They are careful to prepare for the sacrament of the Lord's Supper, and frequent in partaking of it. In Scotland, country parishes have that sacrament dispensed but once a year, and sometimes not so often; but ever since 1742 we have it here twice a year. These have been indeed remarkable times of communion with God: then especially, they have seen the goings of our God and our King in the sanctuary: they have been made to sit under Christ's shadow with great delight, and his fruit has been sweet to their taste: they have been feasted in the banqueting-house, his banner over them was love. And meeting also with like entertainments at communion-occasions' in other places, they resort to many such solemnities in different parts, especially in the season wherein they most abound, as in June, July, and August.

To conclude: They abound much in prayer, both in single or secret prayer, each apart by himself, and in social prayer, jointly with others, not only private, with the family they belong to, and more public and solemn, with the congregation, but in fellowship meetings, or lesser societies that use to meet weekly for prayer and praises to God and christian conference. In 1731, when I came to this parish, there were three of these meetings in it. In 1742 they increased to a dozen or more; now they are decreased to six. In every town or village almost in this side of the country, where there is any competent number of serious lively Christians, and where religion is in a thriving way, there are of these societies for prayer;

and the persevering subjects of the work I speak of, in parishes where any such persons are, always make a part of these societies. Tradesmen, who are member of them, and who work for so much a day, allow their employers to deduct so much from their day's wages as answers to the time they happen to be absent at the meeting for prayer. Some of these societies, besides their ordinary fixed times for meeting, which is usually once a week in the evening, have also their meetings for fasting and prayer upon extraordinary occasions; as sudden tidings of remarkable losses or dangers to any of their concerns, or of events whereby it appears that the interest of religion is in great danger. And sometimes the Lord gives much of his gracious presence and of a spirit of prayer to his people in these, though, alas! not so much as in former times.

I now close with this short caution: If this paper shall fall into the hands of any concerned in the work of which it treats, who shall pervert any thing here said, towards encouraging himself in pride or carnal security, as supposing that he is reckoned here among the persevering subjects of that work; To such I say, perhaps it is not as you imagine; but suppose it be so, what are you the better for that? What was Judas the better for being in the list, and in such repute among the other apostles? Men may approve thee, and God condemn thee: and if thou valuest thyself merely upon the approbation of others, this delusion will ruin thee for ever. Be not high-minded, but fear: those who have indeed been enabled to persevere, and may hope by grace still to persevere in the ways of God, and are the humble and lowly, the modest and self-denied; while the haughty and high-minded, the presumptuous and self-confident, have been suffered to fall, or may expect that a dangerous fall is very near.

"Now to him that is able to keep us from falling, and to present us faultless before the presence of his glory with exceeding joy — to the only wise God our Saviour, be glory and majesty, dominion and power, both now and ever. Amen."

Upon the whole, I think I may say, "The Lord has done great things for us, whereof we are glad." To him alone be all glory and praise, of whatever good was got or done in that remarkable work of his grace. Amen. I am, Your affectionate Brother,

WILLIAM M'CULLOCH.

Chapter 10

The Wind Blows On

It will be agreeable tidings, to all who desire and pray for the coming of the kingdom of God, to be informed that this outpouring of the Holy Spirit is considerably observable to the northward beyond what hath been formerly mentioned in this Narrative. I shall first give some particular account of the remarkable coming of the Comforter to the parish of Muthil, to convince many there of sin, of righteousness, and of judgment.

This parish is situate in the shire of Perth, and presbytery of Auchterarder. They have been many years under the pastoral care of the Rev. Mr. Halley, an able and sufficient minister of the New Testament, and one who is known to be laborious and faithful. The reader will be informed of it much better by a letter I received from the said reverend brother, on the 2nd of this current October, than by any abstract I can give: which letter is as follows:—

Muthil, 28th September, 1742.

Rev. dear Brother, For some time past I have been much refreshed with tidings of great joy, not only from abroad, namely, New-England, and other remote parts, but also from different corners of our land, particularly from the parish whereof you have the pastoral charge,

185

from whence I hear of a gathering of the people to the blessed Shiloh. That you may rejoice with me, and help with your prayers at the throne of grace, I thought it proper to acquaint you with something of the like glorious work in this congregation. I do not in this missive pretend to give you a full and particular account of what the Lord has done amongst us for some time past. In general, for about a year past, there has been an unusual stirring and seeming concern through this congregation, and some now and then falling under convictions. A closer attention to the word preached, and a receiving of it with an apparent appetite, was by myself and others observed, untill the time of the sacrament of the Lord's Supper was dispensed here, which was the third Sabbath of July last, at which time, I think, our conquering Redeemer made some visible inroads upon the kingdom of Satan. I hope there are not a few, both in this and other congregations, that can say, "That God was in this place, and that they felt his power, and saw his glory." But whatever the Lord was pleased to shed down of the influences of his Spirit upon that solemn occasion, comparatively speaking, may be accounted but a day of small things in respect of what gracious God has been pleased to do amongst us since. I must acknowledge, to the praise of our gracious God, that an unusual power hath attended the word preached every Sabbath day since, few if any Sabbaths having passed but some have been awakened, and particularly last Lord's day, which, I hope I may say, was a day of the Son of man in this place; for, besides the general concern that was seen in this congregation, about eighteen persons, which I came to know of that night, were pricked to the heart, and deeply wounded with the arrows of the Almighty, and I expect to hear of a great deal more of them. I have been very agreeably entertained with the visits of distressed souls crying out for Christ, and "What shall we do to be saved?" And I may say, that the work of the law has been severe, and outwardly noticeable upon all that i have conversed with; their convictions have been deep, cutting, and abiding, not (as we have formerly seen) "like a morning cloud and early dew, that soon passeth away." And yet I have not observed in any that I have spoken with the least tendency to despair; but giving, so far as I can judge, satisfying evidences of a kindly work of the Spirit, and the law acting the part of a school-master, leading them to Christ, in whom, I hope, a great many of them are safely landed, and have had their souls filled with joy and peace in believing, and some have received such a measure of the joys of heaven that the narrow crazy vessel could hold no more. Though some old people have been awakened, yet this work is most noticeable among the younger sort: and some very young (within twelve years of age) have been observably wrought upon, and the fruits are very agreeable, amongst others, their delight in prayer and their frequent meeting together for that end. And they who have noticed them have informed me of their speaking in prayer the wonderful things of God. As the Lord has been pleased observably to own us in the public ordinances, and to make us see his goings in the sanctuary, so I think no less have we felt a down-pouring of his Spirit upon the occasion of our evening exercises upon Sabbath nights. For immediately after public worship is over, such crowds of people come to the manse as fill the house and the close before the doors, discovering a great thirst after the word, and such an unusual concern in hearing of it that their mourning cries frequently drown my voice, so that I am obliged frequently to stop till they compose themselves. And many on these occasions fall under deep and abiding convictions. So that I am taken up in dealing with them for some hours after the meeting is dismissed. Many here give such evidences of a saving real work of the Spirit, that to call it into question would put old experienced Christians to doubt of their own state, yea, to call in question the experiences of the saints recorded in Scripture. And yet there are here, as well as elsewhere, who are contradicting and blaspheming; they are objects of pity, and ought to be prayed for. I give you this account of the Lord's work in this parish for your own private satisfaction, and of those with you who may join with us in prayer and praises to our gracious God, who has done such great things for us. We are mindful of you and your congregation, and of the work of God in other parts, not only in public and in private, but in our praying societies, several whereof have been of late erected in this parish, and many people flocking to them. We expect the like from you and your people. That the Lord may carry on his work with you and us, and other parts of the land; and that he may signally countenance that solemn occasion you have in view next Lord's day is the earnest desire and prayer of your affectionate Brother,

WILLIAM HALLEY.

I received, on the 29th of October, a letter from the same worthy brother, giving a further account of the progress of the good work at Muthil. It is a followeth:—

Rev. and very dear Brother, Yours of the 17th instant I received upon the 20th, by which I was exceedingly refreshed with the account of the continuance and progress of the Lord's work in that plot of his vineyard whereof you have the pastoral charge. These things brought about with you here and elsewhere are the doings of the Lord, and wonderful in our eyes, and considering the almost universal deadness, degeneracy, despising of gospel ordinances, slighting the ambassadors of Christ, and the many other crying abominations of the land, this reviving, this surprising visit, may fill us with wonder and amazement, and make us say, "When the Lord returned again the captivity of our Zion we were like men that dream." But "his ways are not as our ways," Glory to him, "He has seen our ways, and is healing them." It gave me much pleasure to hear Mr. Porteous and some of my people giving such an account of the work of God with you at your last sacrament. Such of my flock as attended that solemn occasion, I hope, have not lost their travel. About seven-and-twenty of them, all in a company coming home, were, by a kind providence, overtaken upon the road, by Mr. Porteous, Mrs. Erskine, and Mr. David Erskine, who, by the blessing of the Lord were made eminently useful to them. For such was the distress of many of them, that in all appearance they would have lodged in that desert place all night if the Lord, by means of these instruments, had not sent them some support and relief: so much did their soul-distress affect their bodies that they seemed not able to travel much farther. I doubt not but it will give you like satisfaction to be informed that the same good work upon souls is daily advancing and going on in this parish. Every Sabbath day since I wrote to you last, I may say, to the glory of free grace, has been a day of the Son of man. The arrows of the Almighty King are still flying thick amongst us, and wounding the hearts of his enemies, and laying them down groaning at the feet of the Conqueror, crying under a sense of guilt and the frightful apprehensions of wrath, and thirsting after a Saviour. For many months past, I have observed a general and unusual concern upon the whole congregation, their close attendance upon ordinances, though

189

many of them be at a great distance, their hungry-like attention to the word, the serious and concerned-like airs appearing in their faces. Many being so deeply affected in hearing that frequently a general sound of weeping through the whole congregation rises so high that it much drowns my voice. Their carriage and spiritual converse in comiñg and going from public ordinances, and the many prayers that are put up through this parish, are good and promising appearances, which make me, through the blessing of God upon his ordinances, to expect yet greater things than these I have already seen. I told you in my last, what multitudes of people attended our evening exercise upon Sabbath nights. But now, though the day be short, I am obliged to go to the kirk with them, where almost the whole congregation (which is very great) wait and attend. Many of them not regarding the difficulty of traveling through a long dark moor under night: and a good number after they have heard a lecture and two sermons, and the evening exercise, stay and retire to the school-house, and there spend some hours in prayer, and the Lord has signally owned them, not only to their own mutual edification, but to the conviction of by-standers, and such as have heard them without the walls of the house. Our praying societies are in a most flourishing condition, and still more members flocking to them; their meetings are frequent, and the Lord is observably present with them. The meetings for prayer amongst the young boys and girls give me great satisfaction, one whereof began soon after the sacrament, and is now increased to about the number of twenty. Till of late they met in the town; but several of them fell under such a deep concern that I was sent for to speak with them, where I found some of them in tears. Since that time (that I may have them near me) I give them a room in the manse, where they meet every night. And O how pleasant is it to hear the poor young lambs addressing themselves to God in prayer, with what fervour, with what proper expressions do I hear them pouring out their souls to a prayer-hearing God; so that standing at the back of the door, I am often melted into tears to hear them. We have another praying society of young ones lately erected in another corner of the parish, where one Mr. Robertson teaches one of the charity schools. The young ones of late desired his permission to meet in the school-house for prayer, which he very readily granted to them, (for it is his pleasure to promote and encourage religion both in young and old,) and there about twenty of them met twice every week, though many of them have a good way to travel in the night-time. I may say in general, that such a praying disposition as appears amongst this people, both young and old, was never seen nor heard of before, which gives me ground to expect more of divine influences to come down amongst us, for where the Lord prepares the heart he causes his ear to hear. As to the parish of Madderty, respecting which you desire to be informed; soon after the sacrament at Foulis, a nighbouring parish, some few boys met in the fields for prayer, and when observed, were brought to a house, to whom many others, both young and old, resorted since, and are now, according to my information, in a very flourishing condition. This Presbytery is resolved to divide themselves into societies for prayer, for the progress of this blessed work, and to have frequent meetings for this end. What Perth presbytery hath done I have no certain account of, only I heard what you seem to have been informed of. I will accept of it as a great favour to be allowed a frequent correspondence with you, that we may be mutually informed what the Lord is doing amongst us, and thereby be excited to more diligence in prayer and praises. I am afraid that my last letter to you, wants that politeness and exactness that is proper for a public view; but if the publishing of it may contribute any thing to the spreading of the Redeemer's praises, I allow you to make it a part of your Narrative, though the doing of it may leave some reflection upon me. I hope, though otherwise unacquainted, we shall daily meet at the throne of grace in prayer. That this little cloud, that at first appeared but like a man's hand in the west of Scotland, may spread over the whole land, and send down a plentiful rain to water the whole of the Lord's inheritance amongst us, that the pleasure of the Lord may more and more prosper in your hand, is the earnest prayer of your most affectionate Brother,

WILLIAM HALLEY.

I shall here introduce some of the attestations given to this work by some brethren, who having been for some time here, were witnesses to it, and had much opportunity to converse with several of every sort who were the subjects of it.

In the month of January when I heard last from Muthil, the Rev. Mr. Halley writes, that the work of God was still going on in his congregation, and that there were then several newly awakened, concerning whom he writes that "they appeared to have been touched to the quick, the arrows of the Almighty shot to their very hearts, trembling like the Jailor, crying out against sin, breathing and thirsting after a Saviour. My bowels were moved for them, and I hope the bowels of a compassionate Redeemer were yearning over them, when they were like Ephraim bemoaning themselves. I must tell you as a token for good, a praying disposition among this people not only continues, but is upon the growing hand. Besides what of that is with particular persons and families, our praying societies are encreasing. We have now thirteen of them, and a new one going to be set up. I cannot express how much I am charmed with the young ones. We have now three praying societies of them. One of them, at about two miles distance from this, paid me a most agreeable visit upon the first Monday of the year, a day that young people especially used to be otherwise employed. We had, I think, upwards of forty of them; they continued in prayer and other exercises till about ten at night. But O, to hear the young lambs crying after the great Shepherd! to hear them pouring out their souls with such fervour, with such beautiful expressions, with such copiousness and fulness, did not only strike me with admiration, but melted me down in tears. I wished in my heart that all contradicters, gainsayers, and blasphemers of this work of God had been where I was that night. He also writes that the Rev. Mr. Porteous, minister of Monivaird, told him there was some stirring in his parish.

Since the preceding account was put into the printer's hands, I have received the following later accounts. The Rev. Mr. Halley, in a letter to me of the 29th of March, writes, that the concern in that "congregation continues in hearing the word, though not with such a noise and outcrying as formerly. And though the public awakenings be no so discernible as they were some years ago, yet few Sabbaths pass but we have some pricked in their hearts, and with great anguish of spirit, crying, what shall we do? A law work is still severe and of long continuance with many; but the Lord is supporting, helping them to wait, and keeping them thirsting after relief in Christ. Others who, as I judged, had their wounds bound up, have them fall a-bleeding again; and when the Lord hides his face they are exceedingly troubled, and are almost as much upon the rack as formerly. They are but novices in religion, and know but little of the Lord's ordinary way with his people, which makes them think that there is no sorrow like to their sorrow, no case like theirs. But they will gather experiences, and the Lord will teach them, that he is dealing no otherwise with them than he uses to do with them that love and fear him."

In the parish of Cumbernauld the concern among that people hath continued public and discernible all this winter; there being persons newly awakened from time to time. There is great opposition to the Lord's work in that congregation by the Seceders, and persecution, as far as mocking and the tongue can go, as there is also in the east end of this parish. It is remarkable that the first time the Seceders preached at Cumbernauld, which was in February last, there was a greater stir and more sensible outcry in the congregation at the kirk than had been do some considerable while before. Also, next Lord's-day, when the Seceders had sermon, there was a lad who, when he was entering into the place of their meeting, cast his eye towards the kirk, when this thought came into his mind, What reason can I give for forsaking the minister and following these folk? which troubled him so that he went straight from the place of their meeting to the kirk, where he was awakened and brought to a deep concern about his sinful and lost state. It is also talked that he was carried to the seceding preacher, who advised him to mind and apply himself to his work. A judicious Christian in the bounds having said that was the way Cain took, who went to build cities, suffers their spite for this just thought.

Those in the other parishes to the west of this, who appeared to have got a desirable issue of their awakening, continue to make progress and to walk as becometh Christians, and have the same temptations, doubts, fears, and difficulties that converts in former times had.

The minister of St. Ninians, by a letter to me of the 19th current, writes that "Impressions upon our people are far from wearing off; their behaviour is such as that their enemies themselves cannot quarrel; and hitherto they behave very well — it would give you great pleasure to hear them pray and converse. Our audience is most attentive to the preaching of the word."

The minister of Gargunnock, by a letter to me of the 17th current March, writes, "that the concern there in a great measure continues, their fellowship meetings increase; that even the children's meetings for prayer continue, their outward concern continues even in the public; a diligent attending upon ordinances, love of our God and Redeemer remains, and to all the children of our Lord's family, and especially crying to Christ and rejoicing in him with a sober and blameless conversation." He writes also, "that there are still some under spiritual concern in the parish of Kippen."

There are several hopeful appearances in the Rev. Mr. Porteous's parish of Monivaird, such as an unusual attention to the word, setting up the worship of God in many families where is was formerly neglected, the setting up and increase of praying societies, and a noticeable concern among many young ones, of whom they have two society meetings.

There have also been, for some time past, public and discernible awakenings in the parish of Crieff, where the Rev. Mr. Drummond is minister. Several there have fallen under spiritual trouble and distress. And several praying societies are setting up there.

At Cumbernauld the concern still continues public and discernible, and new awakenings from time to time. I am likewise informed that in the parishes of Kirkintilloch and Campsie there are instances of new awakenings.

Besides the places already mentioned in this Narrative, where there have been or are yet discernible and remarkable awakenings; there are good informations from several other corners concerning various promising tokens for good, which afford probable evidences not only of some success of the gospel, but of superior degrees of success, surpassing former years: such as more careful attendance on sermons both on Sabbath-days and week-days, and on catechising more seriousness in hearing; more inclination to societies for prayer, most remarkably, though not merely, among the younger sort, which seems by the Divine blessing to set others a-thinking; more resort to ministers for private instruction; religion more the subject of conversation; and comfortable accounts given by private Christians, not only to their ministers, but to one another, of the benefit which they hope they reap by the ordinances in their respective congregations; as also earnest longing and much fervent prayer for a greater and more general reviving.

Such comfortable accounts are not only from some country congregations, but from some of the principal cities of this land. At Dundee, meetings for prayer and a praying disposition in them, with Christian knowledge, do still increase. Upon the last week of March they had two new ones set up, so that they have now above twenty of these meetings, and in several of them between twenty and thirty persons. There are also come to my hand certain informations of a promising concern beginning to appear in some congregations in the south-west corner of Fife, besides what has been at Toryburn. I have also lately letters from some of the Lord's people from Angus in the north, and near the borders to the south-east, expressing the most earnest desires and longing for such a reviving in the corners where they dwell.

A PROPOSAL

SUBMITTED TO THE CONSIDERATION OF GOD'S PEOPLE
OF EVERY DENOMINATION.

THAT they agree to meet at the throne of grace every Sabbath morning, in their closets, some time between the hours of seven and nine o'clock, to unite in Prayer for the most important and the most necessary of all blessings.

1st, The outpourings of the Holy Spirit upon the churches of Christ.

2nd, For the spread of the Gospel in its purity and power throughout the world.

Let these be the principal subjects of this social and devout concert for prayer, with which others may be mixed as conveniency may suggest. It will especially be easy to perceive the importance of importunity on such occasions for the interest of Christ in that particular place where Providence has cast our lot, and which is hereby earnestly recommended. And for this purpose, that God's people may be much in prayer for the ministers of Christ in general, and for their own minister or ministers in particular, and they may be assisted and succeeded in the discharge of their high trust. Much need not be said to engage those whose hearts are right with God, to join in this concert for prayer. They will easily recollect that God uniformly represents himself in Scripture as "a God that hears prayer;" and that while he promises the several blessings of the covenant of grace, with blessings of a temporal nature, Ezek. xxxvi, 25, he notwithstanding adds, verse 37, "Thus saith the Lord

198

God, I will yet for this be enquired of by the house of Israel, to do it for them."

It is in answer of prayer God usually imparts any special blessing to his people. Thus prayer becomes both our duty and our privilege. The Christian's own comfort and progress in holiness — the conversion of sinners; and the encouragement and usefulness of the ministers of Christ, are all powerful inducements to a compliance with this proposal, and as such are suggested and urged.

The universal spread of the gospel of Christ in due time, which is the second thing mentioned in the proposed concert, is matter of express and frequent promise in the sacred oracles, and therefore a proper subject of prayer for the people of God in every age, especially extraordinary prayer.

The concert for prayer that is hereby recommended is not a new thing; it has been the practice of pious people in different times and parts of the church, and which God has been pleased to approve by special tokens of his favour.

Who then will join in this duty, so peculiarly necessary in our day?

New-York, May 12, 1806.